This book is presented to

MARK ZIMA

by

EMILY + JACK SMITH

Good-bye High School
Hello College

William H. Willimon

DIMENSIONS
FOR LIVING

NASHVILLE

To William and Harriet,
when they graduate

GOOD-BYE HIGH SCHOOL, HELLO COLLEGE

Copyright © 1992 by Dimensions for Living

This book is printed on recycled, acid-free paper.

Library of Congress Cataloging-in-Publication Data

WILLIMON, WILLIAM H.
  Good-bye high school, hello college / William H. Willimon.
    p.   cm.
  ISBN 0-687-15527-4 (alk. paper)
    1. High school graduates—Prayer-books and devotions English.
  2. College students—Prayer-books and devotions—English.
  I. Title.
  BV4850.W3   1993
  242'.634—dc20   92-15254

Unless otherwise marked, Scripture quotations are from the New Revised Standard Version Bible, Copyright 1989 by the Division of Christian Education of the National Council of the Churches of Christ in the USA. Used by permission.

Scripture quotations marked GNB are from the *Good News Bible*—Old Testament: Copyright © American Bible Society 1976; New Testament: Copyright © American Bible Society 1966, 1971, 1976.

Scripture quotations marked RSV are from the Revised Standard Version of the Bible, copyright 1946, 1952, 1971 by the Division of Christian Education of the National Council of Churches of Christ in the USA. Used by permission.

Scripture quotations marked AP are the author's paraphrase of the Bible.

94 95 96 97 98 99 00 — 10 9 8 7 6 5 4 3 2
MANUFACTURED IN THE UNITED STATES OF AMERICA

❖ Contents

❖ Introduction

These thoughts are written for people, like you, who are graduating or recently have graduated from high school. Whether you call them thoughts, meditations, reflections, or devotionals, they are designed to "get you going"—to get you going and growing in life and your Christian faith as you say good-bye to high school and hello to college.

One of the best things about your life right now is that it is full of beginnings. That's why we call it *commencement, graduation.* You are going forward. Doors are opening. Things are starting to happen. Beginnings are exciting, but beginnings are also a little frightening. How do you know that you will move forward and not backward? It's fine to have new doors to open, but which one is right for you to open?

The thoughts in this book are designed to get you going "on the right foot." They will not explain everything or answer all your questions, but they will put you in the right place to begin. Bible readings begin each meditation and guide the thoughts throughout. Although the key verses for the meditation are printed here for you, you may want to have a Bible handy for additional suggested readings. Some meditations are short, some are long, but all are written with you in mind and the Bible as a guide.

You may choose to read this book alone, perhaps setting aside some special time at the beginning or close of each day. For instance, there are enough meditations here for about three weeks of daily devotionals. Or, you may choose to select meditations as specific needs, questions, or circumstances arise. You also may use these meditations in a small group, asking some people in your dormitory to read and reflect upon the meditations together.

As a pastor who spends much of my day with people at your stage in life, I hope that you will find these thoughts a good beginning for your first weeks in college and the exciting new events happening in your life.

William H. Willimon
Duke University Chapel

❖ Saying Good-bye and Hello

Now faith is the assurance of things hoped for, the conviction of things not seen. Indeed, by faith our ancestors received approval. By faith we understand that the worlds were prepared by the word of God, so that what is seen was made from things that are not visible. (Hebrews 11:1-3)

Read Hebrews 11:8-12; 12:1-2.

You've spent your whole life standing at the door, learning to say good-bye. As a toddler, your parents left you at the door of the nursery. You fought back the tears, bravely trying to wave to them as they left you there. Then there was that first day of school. They walked you as far as the school bus stop, hugged you, and you were gone. Then there was your first time at summer camp, your first visit to far away friends on your own . . . and now this, leaving home after graduation. We call it *graduation* or *commencement,* which are fancy words for that by now familiar experience of standing at the door and saying good-bye.

For you, the door may be opening. Perhaps you feel as if you have lived for this day—glad to be leaving, glad to be beginning a new chapter of your life. You expect to feel free, liberated, excited at the prospect of whatever new place you may be going.

Perhaps you are more impressed with doors closing than with doors opening. Your last day of high school. Your last summer at home. Your last look at friends whom you may never see again.

More than likely, you're both happy and sad. Doors close. Doors open. We say good-bye to the old and hello to the new. As in each new chapter of your life, there is some expectation and excitement, but there is also some sadness and sorrow. Be honest about both the closing and the opening of this new door. Go forward across the threshold grateful for what you have left behind and hopeful for what lies ahead.

Way back, in the book of Genesis, old Abraham and Sarah were asked by God to go forward, to leave their accustomed surroundings and journey, as Paul said, "To a place they knew not." They were much older than you, much more accustomed to the openings and closings of life, and probably all the more apprehensive about what lay ahead for them in this strange, unknown land. Paul says they journeyed in faith, confident that, though they didn't know what the future held for them, they knew who held the future. They believed that God went with them.

Let that be you. You don't know what the future holds for you in the months ahead, how many doors will be opened or closed in your life. But know this: Wherever you go, into whatever unknown places you journey, just like old Abraham and Sarah, God is with you.

❖ What to Take with You

After this the Lord appointed seventy others and sent them on ahead of him in pairs to every town and place where he himself intended to go. He said to them, "The harvest is plentiful, but the laborers are few; therefore ask the Lord of the harvest to send out laborers into his harvest. Go on your way. See, I am sending you out like lambs into the midst of wolves. Carry no purse, no bag, no sandals; and greet no one on the road. What- ever house you enter, first say, 'Peace to this house!' And if anyone is there who shares in peace, your peace will rest on that person; but if not, it will return to you. (Luke 10:1-6)

I hope that you are better at packing than I. One of the tough parts about leaving home to go to college is knowing what to take and what not to take. An extra pair of socks? A tennis racquet? A Bible? I've learned the hard way, on summer trips and vacations, that it's far better to take too little than to take too much. Overloaded suitcases, dragged from here to there, crammed with things that you probably will never need, make for difficult traveling. Experienced travelers learn to pack light.

When Jesus sent out his followers, he told them to travel light. He commanded them not to take purse, bag, or extra sandals. He didn't want them to be burdened by a lot of stuff. Jesus wanted them to be free to devote themselves entirely to the new work he had commissioned them to do.

The journey that you are now on requires care in packing. There is much from home that you will want to take with you: your values, your relationships, your sense of expectation and excitement. But there will be much that you ought to leave behind. Life requires an ability to let go of some old things so that we might grasp new things. Any journey gives us the opportunity to begin new habits and break old ones. We must lay aside past hurts in order that we might be healed. Don't ruin the promise and excitement of the journey you make after high school by trying to take with you everything from the past.

* * *

Take a moment. Get out a pen and paper and make a list of three things that you need to leave behind as you go forth. Then list three new things that you need to take with you.

❖ The Sadness and Joy of Being Alone

[Jesus] went up the mountain by himself to pray. When evening came, he was there alone. (Matthew 14:23b)

I remember my first week of college as a good time, but also as a time of loneliness. There were lots of people at the orientation sessions, people at parties, people in the cafeteria at meals, everyone talking, laughing, everyone trying to make a good first impression on everyone else. As you know, sometimes a crowd can be the loneliest place to be. You get the feeling that everyone else knows what they are doing, everyone but you.

You may know lots of people where you are going to college, but when it comes down to it, you are there alone. You have to make it or break it by yourself. It can be frightening, cut off, away from parents, lifetime friends, family. There will be times when others fail to include you in their plans and parties. There will be times when, even though they try to include you, you will still feel very much alone. Your values are different from theirs. Your ideas of what is right and what is wrong will make you a "loner." Loneliness is no one's idea of a good time.

There is another side to our aloneness, a better side. It consists of those moments in life when we are glad to be alone. Your roommate leaves for the weekend and you are all by yourself for three days, and it is wonderful! Everyone else goes out for the evening but you stay behind, grateful for the chance to be with yourself and your thoughts, pleased by the quiet and the peace. This is the joy of being alone.

Life is best as an alternating rhythm of times of engagement and detachment. Time with others, time by yourself.

Jesus knew this. His life was an active one, a very public ministry with crowds pressing in upon him, controversy swirling around him. He also knew the loneliness of being misunderstood, betrayed by friends, mocked by others. In the end, he died very much alone.

Yet Jesus was able to live and die as he did because he also knew the *joy* of being alone. He began his ministry alone, in the wilderness, wrestling with what God wanted him to do with his life, struggling against the temptation to be someone he was not. Throughout his ministry, there were times when he left the crowds, as well as his disciples and went away to pray. Surely these times alone gave Jesus the strength to go back renewed and rededicated, refreshed for his work.

In all your activity at college, set aside some time each week to be alone, to pray, to reflect, or to do nothing in particular. The best way to be with others, is first to have learned to be by yourself.

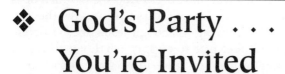

❖ God's Party . . . You're Invited

> *"But the father said to his slaves, 'Quickly, bring out a robe—the best one—and put it on him; put a ring on his finger and sandals on his feet. And get the fatted calf and kill it, and let us eat and celebrate; for this son of mine was dead and is alive again; he was lost and is found!' And they began to celebrate."* (Luke 15:22-24)

Read Luke 15:11-32.

Each of us attempts to make sense out of life through stories. If we can't tell a story about ourselves, then we are nothing more than detached bundles of facts, dates, and faces signifying nothing. Every people makes sense of itself through certain "master stories." Ancient Greece, for example, listened to Homer's tale of Odysseus who left home and ventured on a wide dark sea.

In Homer's story, Odysseus' son, Telemachus, realized that, with his old man away on business for some time, he must grow up and take charge of things at home. Eventually, Odysseus returned, but not before Telemachus had to stand on his own two feet—which the Greeks defined as wisdom.

Jesus told another story; it was a story of a father and two sons. In Jesus' story, it was a *son* who left home, traveled to the "far country," and finally came to his senses and returned home. The father waited for the son to come to his senses and return home—which Jesus defined as wisdom.

The Greeks wondered what to do when one is abandoned by the father. Jesus pondered life as a problem of never being able to be rid of the Father.

A younger son says, "Father, give me my inheritance." (In other words, "drop dead," for there is no other way to put the old man's will into effect.) And the old man does just that. Out in the "far country" Jesus says the boy engaged in "loose living." (Though Jesus doesn't define "loose living," feel free to supply whatever forms of "loose living" appeal to you—loose girls, loose boys, chocolate cake.) Eventually the boy "comes to himself." He comes back to himself, saying, "Wait a minute. I don't have to starve out here. I have a father, a home." And he turns back toward home.

The boy has written a little speech for the occasion. "Now look, Dad, before you start yelling, let me explain why she answered the phone when you called my room," or "Dad, er, uh, I mean, Father, I have sinned. I am unworthy to be called your son. Treat me as one of your hired servants."

But the father isn't interested in speeches.

"Chill it," says the father. "Come on in. I'll show you a real party."

Which is why this story has always been a shocker. We

14

thought Jesus came to jack up ethical standards, to put a bit more muscle into our moral fiber. Yet, here the homecoming of a ne'er-do-well is *a party*. It isn't what we expect. We want the father to be gracious, but not overly so. Our question is that of the older brother, "Is it fitting to throw a party for a prodigal?"

What we want is, "Yes, Howard, glad that you're back home. Now let's do away with that earring and let's have a bit more responsibility out of you. Go in, have a good, balanced meal and then let's talk about finishing your application to law school. Okay, Howard?"

But this is not what we get. What we get is a story about a *party*, thrown by a father for a prodigal. Why does Jesus, in telling this story, expend more verses describing the party than on any other single aspect in the story?

Let me remind you of the story's context. One day Jesus' critics cried, "You eat and drink [that is, party] with *sinners*! What kind of Savior are you?" We expect Jesus to back off and say, "But I'm going to redeem these whores and tax collectors! Make 'em straighten up, be more responsible, like you and me." But no. Jesus tells them that God loves to party with sinners. He tells of a series of parties when a woman found a lost coin, a bash after finding a lost sheep, followed by the biggest, most questionable blow-out of all, the party for the prodigal son. The son returns, the father throws a party, and they begin to make merry. End of scene one.

Now enters our favorite character in the story—the older brother.

Nostrils flared, look of indignation: "Music! Dancing! Levity! and on a Wednesday! What are you doing in that tux?" he asks the servant.

"Your kid brother's home. The old man has given everybody the night off and there's a party."

The older brother is angry and won't go in. The father comes out into the darkness and begs him to come party.

"Come on in, Ernest," says the father. "So what, you're

15

the biggest farmer in the county. Big deal. Come on in. Let's party."

As it turns out, the most interesting character in the story is not the prodigal son or the older brother. It's the father. He's the real prodigal, in that his love is extravagant, more excessive than either the younger brother's loose living or the older brother's moral rectitude.

This is a story about a parent who is excessive in his persistence to have a family, an old man who meets us when we drag in from the far country after good times go bad or who comes out to the lonely dark of our righteousness and begs us to come in and party.

This is also a story about what it's like to be claimed. The younger brother is well known to us in our families. He is the person who is always gasping for air, threatening to leave—and sometimes leaving. In each of us, there is a person who is gasping, reaching for space, kicking at the bounds. The older brother is also known to us. He is the always dutiful and thoughtful one who is caring, concerned, and eventually filled with great resentment. Every family has someone who carries so much of the moral weight that, after awhile, he or she just feels used and gets tired of other people not shaping up. Everybody gets tired of being responsible all the time.

But this is mainly a story about the father. Finally both sons must deal with the father. On the one hand, he gives both sons what they need. He lets the younger son come back to the family. He also gives to the older brother what he needs—reassurance: "You are always with me. Everything I've got is yours."

On the other hand, the father does not give the sons what they want. The younger son says, "Make me just one of your hired hands." But the father says, "No, I'm not going to do that. You will have to act responsibly." The older son wants a party, but the father says, "No, you're not going to get a party. What you're going to get is everything, including your brother."

16

G. K. Chesterton said that there are two ways to get home. One is to go away and come back; the other is never to leave. There is a push and pull inside us, conflict between wanting to go and resenting that we stayed. The story says that there is also a push and pull outside us: God. It is the Father who waits for one to come home and the other to come party. The story begins and ends with the Father.

The story's claim that God is the parent who refuses to stop silently waiting or earnestly pleading collides with modern self-understanding that our lives are our possessions, like a car, to do with as we please. Our society has initiated you into a world of "the individual." We have suggested that there is no way for you to grow up without severing ties, putting parents, values, and community behind. Our universities sever your ties with your parents only to abandon you to the most totalitarian group of all—namely, people like you.

Homelessness has become the image of our culture, a culture in which intense loneliness is a byproduct of a people determined to be free of all attachments save the most debilitating attachment of all—enslavement to ourselves. The story, however, suggests that life begins, not in our being free, but in our having a claim laid upon us. "Your brother is home," or "Son, all that I have is yours."

The story is about the way to true wisdom. Not the conventional modern tale of a journey deeper, ever deeper, into the recesses of your own ego, for that's a way not to grow but to shrink. Rather, it's a story about two boys, brothers, who had a father. Without the father there is no family, no story. The old man loves both boys and is determined to love them in ways that do not abandon them to their own devices.

Paradoxically, to know who owns you, claims you, is to know true freedom. If you don't know to whom you belong, who it is who awaits you, you're apt to be the willing victim of anybody blowing through town who promises some means of overcoming your sense of emptiness. When you stand before the powers of the corporation or the conformist pressures of the group, it is freedom to know that they don't own you.

Please note that the story doesn't have an ending. We are not told if the younger brother ever "grew up" or if the older brother ever came in and joined the party. We doubt that they "lived happily ever after." Jesus doesn't end the story because this is a story that you finish yourself. And you are finishing it, for the one on whom Jesus is waiting, or the one whom he is begging to come in and party, is *you*. You have now graduated, commenced into the world. Whether you are glad or sad about your commencement, this story says, *you journey not alone*. There is One who names you, claims you, has plans for you, waits or prods, invites or blesses you. And this One will sooner or later have you!

❖ On Growing Up

> Then I said, "Ah, Lord GOD! Truly I do not know how to speak, for I am only a boy." But the LORD said to me,
> "Do not say, 'I am only a boy';
> for you shall go to all to whom I send you,
> and you shall speak whatever I command you."
> Jeremiah 1:6-7

Read Jeremiah 1:1-9; I Corinthians 13:11-12.

Isn't it odd? You have spent so much of your life wanting to be treated like an adult, wishing your parents would stop acting as if you were still a child, waiting until the time when you could be grown-up. Now, you've got your chance and you're not altogether sure if you want to be an adult or not.

It's good at last to have the freedom to be on your own, making more of your own decisions, guiding the direction of your own life. But along with that come lots of dilemmas. Despite your conflicts with your parents over the course of your life, aren't there times when, at least in the back of your mind, you secretly wish they were here to tell you what to do, to send you back to your room to study, to insist that you go to bed when you ought, to tell you whether or not this or that is right or wrong for you?

You have at last got what you wanted—freedom, independence, responsibility for your life—and now realize that it's all up to you. That's scary. You can't blame anybody for how things work out now. It's all up to you. There are now no more, "If only you had let me. . . . " or "If you had just told me. . . . " Welcome to adulthood.

When he was young, about your age, Jeremiah heard God ask him to go speak to the king, to say to the people what God wanted them to do. Jeremiah at last had his chance to grow up. His response? "Lord, I don't know how to speak; I am too young" (Jeremiah 1:6 GNB).

God told Jeremiah to grow up.

Welcome to adulthood. The same God who has loved when you were still in the womb (see Jeremiah 1:5) continues to love you into your future, has big plans for you, and walks with you into your tomorrow.

❖ God's Way or Your Way?

The devil said to him, "If you are the Son of God, command this stone to become a loaf of bread." (Luke 4:3)

Read Luke 4:1-13.

As a young man, Jesus was led into the wilderness. There, the devil met him and tempted him. It is fitting that we recall this story right after your high school graduation because it is at the beginning of your adult life when you are most preoccupied with the question "Who am I?"

The who-am-I identity question is behind this strange, shadowy meeting with the devil in the wilderness. And I suppose many of you can relate to Jesus in his temptation. Have you ever felt "tempted" to walk down a path toward a future that is not really yours? I would bet that there are a number of you who are wrestling right now with a parent who wants you to go to medical school while you think that you should study dance. The folks at home want you to join the family business, but you have your heart set on teaching history. Well, who are you, anyway? Who tells you who you are? A place to begin is to ask these questions of Jesus.

Who tells Jesus who he is? In chapter 3 of his Gospel, Luke recounts Jesus' baptism. The heavens open and a voice from heaven says, "You are my Son, the Beloved" (3:22). Here, fasting in the wilderness, is Emmanuel, Messiah, God's only begotten.

But *what kind of Messiah is Jesus?* What kind of God are we getting in Jesus? Luke helps us to answer by revealing, in this story of the temptation, who Jesus is.

"If you are really the long-awaited Messiah," said Satan, "Let's see some sign of it. You're hungry after your forty-day fast? So are lots of other people who spend their whole lives without a decent meal. If you are God, make these stones into bread. After all, what could be more compassionate, more godly, than mercy upon hungry people?"

Jesus responds: "It is written, we shall not live by bread alone."

Satan tries again. "Feeding the hungry doesn't appeal to you? Well, I can see your point. Feed the hungry today; what good does that do tomorrow? Let's feed them forever! How? Through the only long-term means of good we know—politics. Here, laid out before you, are all the kingdoms of the world. I will give you power over

20

them and their glorious accomplishments (because, after all, I own them—politics is my major area of satanic concern). All you must do is recognize my authority. Worship me."

Jesus responds: "It is written, we shall worship only one God."

"Well," Satan continues, "if you won't show a little compassion for the hungry, if you don't really care about making the world a better place in which to live, then at least show a little concern for those struggling to believe, who can't believe. Show that crowd down there in the pews that you are indeed who the voice said you are. Leap from the chapel tower and stand before them unbroken. After all, you're God."

Jesus replies: "It is said, you shall not tempt the Lord your God."

Now what do you make of this strange story? An obvious response is that the story of Jesus' temptation encourages us in our own temptations. Jesus resisted temptation. We should resist as well. And who has more temptations than college students?

Beware of the Bible being obvious. It's obvious that we need help in our struggles with temptation. What may not be obvious is how the Bible names temptation. Therefore, I want you to think of this story as a story about how *we* tempt Jesus, about how you and I are determined to make him into a Messiah more in tune with our own assessment of our needs.

The Bible finds uninteresting the modern infatuation with the question "Is there a God?" The Bible's chief concern is, *"What kind of God is there?"* Adam and Eve, the very first people, are the first to trip over the question. Being told that they are built "in the image of God," Adam and Eve quite naturally assume that God must obviously be concerned about meeting their needs. They are hungry, not just for food, but also for life, for knowledge. So, when they "saw that the tree was good for food, and . . . a delight to the eyes, and that the tree was to be desired to make one wise" (Are not food, beauty, and wisdom worthy human goals?), they ate the fruit of the one tree that God had forbidden (Genesis 3:6).

And after liberation from Egyptian slavery, once free and out in the wilderness, the Hebrew children's first demand of God was for food. They said to Moses, "God should have killed us like he killed the Egyptians rather than to bring us out here in the middle of nowhere with no food" (Exodus 16:3 AP). God gave them food, manna.

So, when you hear the devil taunt Jesus with "if you are the Son of God, command this stone to become bread," remember that you have heard it before. Temptation is a function of hunger. Is God for us or not? they asked Moses. Let's have bread as proof that God is our kind of God, a God who responds to our hungry need. What good is religion or praying, or your getting out of bed and going to church if it is not *effective,* if it doesn't yield *results* in your life? "We have forsaken everything and followed you," the disciples said to Jesus. "Now, what's in it for us?"

When Satan enters the story and has an opportunity to tell his side, this seems to be his main theme. "If you are really God," says Satan, "make bread, minister to their hunger. Because that's really the object of their worship, the real reason they fall on their knees, put their dollars in the plate, wear gold crosses around their necks—bread."

Once we realize God can't lower himself to give us always what our hearts desire, we wonder why God at least can't give us a sign. What's the harm in a *sign?* A believer looks at a butterfly emerging from the cocoon and says, "See, there's your proof of God!" A nonbeliever looks at the same cocoon and says, "See, there's your universe working quite fine, thank you, with no need of fairy tales about God." And you know, the world appears to be set up just that way. You can read it as: This is my

22

Father's world. You can read it as: This is an amazing series of cosmic accidents. Why not a clear, unambiguous sign?

"This shall be a sign unto you," we read at Christmas. "You shall find the babe wrapped in swaddling clothes, lying in a manger." But there is so much post-Christmas pain. There's your sign. Yes, God is with us. No, God has gone. Nothing crude like manna from heaven. Just a sign is all we ask.

"Teacher, we want a sign," they said. "An evil and adulterous generation seeks a sign" (Luke 11:29) was his reply.

Well, who do we say that he is? The heavenly voice, at his baptism, said that he was the only begotten Son of God. But he just stands there, quoting scripture, giving us neither bread nor a sign, grasping neither political power to change the world nor even making bread to feed the world. "If you are the son of God. . . ."

It's a big *if* that Satan poses and Jesus does so little to remove it. If you are the Son of God. . . .

Well, who do we say that he is? Jesus put that to his disciples. Who do people say that I am? Peter's hand was the first to go up. "You are the Messiah of God" (Luke 9:20). At last we shall get this movement organized, unfurl the banners, and get this messiah thing going!

No. "He sternly ordered and commanded them to tell no one, saying, ' The Son of Man must undergo great suffering, and be rejected . . . , and be killed.'" (9:22)

Matthew has a bit more to say about this episode than Luke. Matthew has Peter blurt out, "God forbid, Lord!" God forbid that you should be a God who is rejected, suffers, and finally dies just like us. What good is a God like that? No bread, no sign, no power, no glory! And Matthew says that Jesus turned to Peter (who is there for us) and says, "Get behind me, Satan!"

Can you see? We have been asking, have we not, who is this God, and who is his only Son, whom we are to love?

23

And Jesus turns our question back upon us. *Who is this Satan*, this demonic tempter who is bent on tripping me up, tempting me to walk a path other than the one God has commanded? Don't you see? The Satan, the tempter, *is one of Jesus' own disciples!* The ones who offer Jesus the greatest temptation, who are desperate to transform him, are his own people—us. The temptation he resists is *us!* If we want to look for the devil, we ought first to look among ourselves—Jesus' own people who, rather than follow on his terms, attempt to make him over into our own image of who God ought to be rather than to follow him as the God the Scriptures say he is.

The good news is, he is able to resist temptation in the wilderness or in our church. Get thee behind me, Satan! He not only quotes Scripture, he lives the Scriptures, embodies, in his own life, the God of whom the Scriptures speak. Later, they tempted him even as he hung in agony upon the cross: "If you are the Chosen of God, save yourself." This time he didn't quote Scripture, he just hung there. Sometimes, when we ask him to be our kind of God rather than the God he is, sometimes, in love, he is silent.

It's hard to hear our Lord curse us, and demand that we get behind him as he moves down the dark, narrow way toward the cross. The good news is that he walks it for us, despite us, because of us. It is also our way, this way of the cross. And the good news arising out of his triumph over temptation is that he will go ahead and be God. This Messiah is neither inclusive nor pliable. If he would go on and save us, he must first be able to hold out against us and our demands. He will go ahead and be a real God, not some projection of our egos. Not our will but *thine* be done.

Don't just do something, Jesus, *stand there.* Stand there for us, faithful even when we are not, true to Scripture. Be the God for us we don't deserve and didn't ask for. Despite us, don't just do something, stand there.

❖ Habits of the Heart

"So I say to you, Ask, and it will be given you; search, and you will find; knock, and the door will be opened for you." (Luke 11:9)

Read Luke 11:1-13.

Now that you are finished with high school and may be leaving home, many of your old, accustomed routines may be disrupted. Without parents to get you up on Sundays for church, without your mother to tell you to eat your vegetables, without someone standing over you to have you do your homework—you may find yourself neglecting some important matters.

Too often, we think of religion as a spontaneous matter of having the right emotions, the proper feelings. Either you feel like it or you don't. Yet some things in life, often the most important things, are best not left to chance. Your relationship with God is something that requires time, effort, persistence. At least that is what Jesus seemed to be saying in his parable about the friend at midnight.

In the middle of the night, a man realizes that he has no bread. So he goes and knocks on his neighbor's door to ask for a loaf. The neighbor is in bed and tells him to get lost. But the man is persistent. He keeps knocking, banging on the door until his neighbor finally gets up, opens the door, and gives him some bread so the knocking will stop. This is the way we ought to pray, says Jesus.

Prayer takes persistence. Not because God will not open the door until I knock it down. Usually, the problem with our relationship with God is that the doors of our hungry hearts are closed to God, shut to God's repeated attempts to be open to us! So we must keep knocking and keep praying, mind our habits of the heart because the door I am trying to open is my own. The one who is more earnestly seeking is God, and the one who is most oblivious to the knocking at the heart's door is I!

* * *

Take a moment and think about two or three specific things you can do to cultivate the presence of God in your life:

Read the Bible daily. _____

Pray daily. _____

Attend church regularly. _____

Join a campus prayer group. _____

Become active in your denominational student group
    on campus. _____

Read a book on a Christian theme. _____

Set aside time each day for quiet reflection. _____

Other: _____

❖ Burdens as Blessings

> *"Come to me, all you that are weary and are carrying heavy burdens, and I will give you rest. Take my yoke upon you, and learn from me; for I am gentle and humble in heart, and you will find rest for your souls. For my yoke is easy, and my burden is light."* (Matthew 11:28-30)

Vacations are wonderful opportunities to "get away from it all." A period of time, set aside from life's daily difficulties, when we unburden. Where there have been alarm clocks, there is now sleeping until ten. God bless vacations . . . marvelous, unburdening.

Jesus needed a vacation. In the Galilean cities, he experienced little but rejection. In great fatigue and desperation, Jesus blew his top. "To what shall I compare this generation? You are like a bunch of children" (Matthew 11:16-19 AP). He told all those cities who rejected him that, on the judgment day, when God finally gives them what they deserve, it will be no better for them than it was for Sodom (Matthew 11:20-24).

It wasn't one of Jesus' better moments. But he was tired, tired of rejection, exhausted by hard work without results, dead tired. He needed a summer break, a time to unburden, a vacation.

> At that time Jesus said . . . [at that time, right after he revealed his own exhaustion], "Come to me, all you that are weary and are carrying heavy burdens, and I will give you rest. Take my yoke upon you, and learn from me; . . . and you will find rest for your souls. For my yoke is easy, and my burden is light." (Matthew 11:25, 28-30)

These are some of the most beloved of all Jesus' words. "Come to me, all who labor and are heavy laden." Here is an invitation to vacation. Sabbath in the deepest sense of the word.

In even the most invigorated life, there comes that day when our enthusiasm dulls and our excitement dissipates. Sometimes even religion is a burden. Going to church and reading the Bible can become tiresome, no more than a duty, a habit, kept going by inertia rather than commitment.

This probably was the burden of which Jesus was speaking. Jesus later complained about how religious leaders placed heavy burdens on people's backs and would not lift a finger to remove them (Matthew 23:4). The blessing of religion can become a burden. Religion reduced to *should, ought, must.* There are those who spend their whole lives getting over the damage done by "religion."

In another episode in Matthew's Gospel, Jesus' disciples walk through a grainfield one Sabbath. They are hungry so they pluck some grain. "Look!" cried Jesus' critics, "your disciples are doing what it is unlawful to do on the Sabbath!" Jesus replies that the critics have perverted religion. God wants mercy, not sacrifice (Matthew 12:1-8).

You can, no doubt, think of other examples of the way Jesus unburdened people from oppressive religion.

"Come to me, all who labor and are heavy laden, and I will give you rest. Take my yoke upon you, and learn from me."

Wait a minute. Did Jesus say *"yoke"*? Do you find it surprising that Jesus offers tired, burdened people what they seem least to need? What labored, heavy laden folk need is a vacation, not a yoke. A yoke is a work instrument used to help oxen pull loads. Jesus' yoke may be "easy" and his burden "light," but a yoke is still a yoke and a burden is still a burden. Just when we expect Jesus to offer us a vacation, he offers us a yoke different from the one around our necks, a burden other than the one we are currently bearing. Instead of escape, Jesus offers tired people new equipment. A burden. A yoke.

Whatever the deliverance Jesus offers, it is not deliverance from responsibility or accountability. Martin Luther noted that only Jesus could say, "Come to me all you who are heavy laden" in one breath, and "I will place around your necks a yoke" in the next breath (*Luther's Works*, 7:837-38)! Perhaps Jesus dares to speak of giving us rest by placing his burden upon us because he knows that the issue in life is not *if* we shall be burdened but rather *which burdens we shall bear.*

As a pastor, I spend much of my day providing comfort to people who are cracking under the burdens of affluence. Two cars, the big mortgage. So many of our emotional, physical illnesses are due to stress brought on by economic overextension.

"Honey, the dishwasher is not working. By the way, the hot water heater is on the blink. Wait here until the garage door repairman calls." There are weeks when we appear to be the victims of a revolt of appliances and gadgets. We bought all this stuff to free us, to unburden our lives. How ironic that we end up servicing our machines rather than our machines serving us. I wait for the plumber to arrive, therefore I am. Take my ten years of installment payments upon you, for my yoke is easy and my burden is light.

Life's greatest burden is not in having too much to do (some of the happiest folk I know are the busiest) but in having nothing worthwhile to do. Energy is a renewable resource. Good work appears to produce energy to do more good work. People seem to "burn out" not because they have too much to do but because they become exhausted by constant engagement with the trivial and the inconsequential.

So the issue before us cannot be *if* we shall be burdened, but to *what* shall we be burdened? Not *if* we shall be yoked, but to *whom*?

Jesus appears to have no interest in unburdening us so that we can be free, or liberated, or assured by self-esteem or all those other modern infatuations that are themselves such debilitating burdens. Jesus lifts one burden off our backs so he can place another; he removes the harness we forge for ourselves so that he can place around our necks his own yoke.

Jesus' idea of a good vacation is not "getting away from it all," but taking us someplace where we are given something significant to do—namely, participation with him in his ministry to the world. "Make me a *captive*, Lord, and then I shall be *free*." That's how one hymn puts it.

Marriage is a good example of this idea. Sometimes we think of a marriage as a limitation. It is limiting, burdensome to be so closely yoked to another human being, to limit one's intimacies to one person, to be forced to account for one's movements. But often one awakes to the realization that what one earlier perceived as a limitation or burden becomes true freedom, great joy. In marriage, one is free from the little games, the masks one must wear before others. Now, since fidelity is promised forever, no matter what, the promise of marriage has freed us rather than restricted us. What was once perceived as a burden is really a great blessing.

More than this, by keeping the promises of marriage, we discover that we have become more complex, interesting persons ourselves. In taking on the burden of the promise to be faithful to another person, we have become faithful people so that later in marriage we do not have to say, "Now remember, I promised to be faithful to this other person. I've got to try hard to bear the burden of fidelity." We are faithful, without even having to think about it. In bearing the burden of fidelity, we have become faithful in such a way that it really isn't a burden anymore. Now, it's the way we are. This yoke is easy. This burden is light.

I pray for you, for you who are plowing through these words when you could just as well be on vacation. I pray, not that Jesus will deliver you of all burdens and free you from all yokes, but that he will give you a burden worth bearing and a yoke worth wearing.

Make me a captive, Lord, then I shall be truly free.

❖ Choices

For to me to live is Christ, and to die is gain. . . . Yet which I shall choose I cannot tell. I am hard pressed between the two. My desire is to depart and be with Christ, for this is far better. But to remain in the flesh is more necessary on your account. (Philippians 1:21-24 RSV)

Read Philippians 1:12-24.

"Why do you enjoy preaching at a university chapel?" the interviewer asked. And I heard myself reply, "Because it's a great privilege to be around young adults, students, who are making so many important decisions in their lives. The way I see it, of the five or six most important choices we make—choices about career, education, marriage—many of them will be made right here. And I enjoy preaching to and counseling with people who are at that stage of life."

It is a privilege to be with people who are pondering such questions as What ought I to do with my life? With whom am I in love? It is especially good to be with students who have so many talents and abilities and therefore, so many interesting choices. Should I go into clinical work or concentrate on research? Should I go to graduate school to study French or Law? Should I marry the cattle rancher from Wyoming or the film producer from L.A.?

You and I live in an age that revels in the glory of choice. Never have we Americans enjoyed so many different opportunities and alternatives as we do now. Think of your grandparents, your great-grandparents, particularly your great-grandmother. More than likely, when she was your age, life was a lot less complicated because there were fewer choices. The majority of people followed a path already well-trod by their parents before them. Then, there wasn't this great agony of what to do with life. There were few options, less freedom, and, we think, less satisfaction in life because of scarcity of alternatives.

You and I are apt to judge the happiness and success of our lives on the basis of how many choices we enjoy. Today, a woman is no longer limited to that narrow range of socially acceptable occupations; she can choose. And because she can choose, she seems more complete. It's difficult to think of someone as a fulfilled human being, living up to his or her full potential, when the person has little or no choice.

How did you choose your husband? "Well, only one man ever spoke to me and so that one was the one I had to marry." How did you decide to go into the ministry?

"Well, I was going to be a scientist, but I flunked algebra in the eighth grade, so that narrowed it down to either law or the ministry, and then, when I did poorly in history, I ended up in seminary." What kind of reason is that? What kind of humanity is that?

My choice is the exercise of my highest human capacity. I am not a vine, clinging to whatever happens to be closest to where I was planted. I'm not a piece of flotsam, bobbing along the stream of life. I am here because I *decided* to be here. I took this road and not that one. This is what I want to do and chose to do.

But what are we to make of the rather confused testimony of a prisoner named Paul? Who can be any less free, any more devoid of choice, and therefore of true humanity, as we define it, than a person in prison? His letter to the Philippians was written near the end of his life, when Paul was awaiting execution in a Roman jail.

"I want you to know, beloved that what has happened to me has actually helped to spread the gospel, so that it has become known throughout the whole imperial guard" (Philippians 1:12-13).

Paul can be forgiven this bit of hyperbole. The leader of the church is in jail. Caesar has him. If Caesar has Paul, Caesar must have the church as well, for as Paul goes, so goes the church. "He's just trying to make us feel better about this defeat," they must have said in Philippi with a stiff upper lip.

Here's a man in jail. No power over his destiny. No way to go forward or to pull back. No choice. Paul has gotten to talk theology with a couple of Roman G.I.'s. Big deal. If he still had choices, some way to get over or around or out of this predicament, then perhaps Paul could talk about the advance of the gospel, but not here in jail.

We have said that life is full only when there is choice, alternative, possibility, freedom. And yet, Paul's letter reminds us, there is a good deal of life that's lived where there are no choices, no alternatives.

Think about how many of the things that make you the way you are, are matters over which you had absolutely no decision, no choice at all. Your name, your gender, your physical appearance, your accent.

Harvard professor Eric Erickson says that a person's ability to trust is developed in the first six weeks of life. If, for some reason, the world appears to be untrustworthy to the infant of six weeks, Erickson believes that child's level of trust may be damaged for life. Child developmentalists say that a child learns half of everything it will ever know in life in the first three years of life! Socially, politically, emotionally, intellectually, so many things lie outside the realm of my decision.

Let's speak frankly: For most of our lives, we are not dealing among a host of alternatives but deciding what to do with what we already have, what to do when there is *no* alternative.

What are you to do then?

You can shake your fist at heaven and rage, say the world is out of joint. You can crawl off under a rock somewhere and howl at the injustice, the unfairness of it all; distort your face into a frown and offer unsolicited cynical comments about life; turn your voice into a whine.

"Oh, I wanted to, but, you see my father never let me. . . ."

"I could have, if my boyfriend had let me, but he just forbade me to. . . ."

"The professor was down on me from the first, never gave me a. . . ."

Paul writes from jail:

> I shall rejoice. For I know that through your prayers and the help of the Spirit of Jesus Christ this will turn out for my deliverance. . . . Christ will be honored . . . whether by life or by death. For to me to live is Christ, and to die is gain. . . . Yet which I shall choose I cannot tell. I am hard pressed between the two. (Philippians 1:18*b*-23 RSV)

33

Wait a minute. "Which I shall choose?" What is this? Paul is in prison. He is neither judge nor jury. What possible meaning could there be in his choice? Perhaps prison has disoriented his mental capacities.

Or perhaps, just perhaps, Paul is saying that, by the Spirit of Jesus, *there is a way when there is no way.*

❖ You're Not Alone

> The spirit of the Lord GOD is upon me, because the LORD has anointed me; he has sent me to bring good news to the oppressed, to bind up the brokenhearted, to proclaim liberty to the captives, and release to the prisoners. (Isaiah 61:1)

Read Isaiah 61:1; Acts 8:14-17; Luke 3:15-22.

When Jesus was baptized in the muddy Jordan as a young man, the heavens cracked open and fire descended upon him like a dove. John had predicted as much: "I wash you with water. The one who is mightier is coming to burn you with fire." Thus began Jesus' work.

His earthly ministry culminates with the Risen Christ coming back to his disciples and telling them, "You wait in Jerusalem until I give you the same power which I have" (Acts 1). Then, on the day of Pentecost, the heavens open again, there is a rush of wind and flames of fire.

That baptismal fire has, since Pentecost, spread like wildfire over the face of the earth so that there is no nation anywhere without people who are empowered with the same power that inflamed Jesus. Across all boundaries—racial, national, political—leapt this fire; this fire has pushed through all barriers so that, in every corner of the earth, there is someone who is able to rise up and say, "The Spirit of the Lord GOD is upon me, because the LORD has anointed me; he has sent me to bring good news to the oppressed, to bind up the brokenhearted, to ers" (Isaiah 61:1). Power. Fire. Spirit.

He was born and bred, as they say, in North Carolina. Natural for him were two water fountains in stores, one marked Colored, the other marked White. The other people never had last names, only Sam or Mary, Sadie, or worse, Buck, Uncle, Boy, Girl. They never entered by the front door, sat only at the back of the bus, drank only from mayonnaise jars when they worked in the yard.

But that was yesterday, a long time ago, mistakes made by his parents, not him. He now lived in the New South where things were done differently. Yes, differently, which means more subtly, covertly.

They sat in big, leather-bound chairs around the great oak table in the boardroom. He had worked hard to sit there, around that table.

"It's not that I dislike her," said the boss. "It's just that, it's just that she really doesn't quite fit in. She's not one of us, if you know what I mean."

Everybody knew what he meant, but nobody said it. Everybody reached down deep, deep in the past, to dredge up all those unstated, unwritten, but sealed-in-concrete customs and mores that told you who you were and defined the boundaries between us and them.

But for some reason, he reached even deeper, past the prejudices, and he said, "Jack, you know, and we all know that's not right. She has done the work. She deserves the promotion. This company ought to set the standard for fair dealings with our people—regardless of the color of their skin."

Power. Power not of his own creation.

She wanted—wanted more than anything—love. She was so lonely, going every evening, at the end of every single evening, home to a place that didn't feel like home, a forlorn, empty, cold apartment. Out of her loneliness she began to visit bars, not to drink, but out of desperation for a place to meet. There she met other lonely ones. At last she met someone and they talked and it was won-

35

derful. They had so much in common. And she said to herself, "This is what it can be like. Two people, adult, sharing."

Then he said to her, in an unspoken way that said it all, that they should share something more than their opinions and conversation. And she was afraid. In that moment, she knew that she might risk losing him, a chance for companionship, love. But from somewhere, in a split-second, she found the means to say, "No. I'm not ready for that yet." She, as it turned out, was not alone. Spirit. Spirit empowering her to be more than she could have been on her own.

Jesus promised us, "Just wait. I'll give *you* the same power that has encouraged me."

Near the end of John's Gospel, as Jesus prepares to go to his cross, he tells his grieving disciples, "I will not leave you comfortless. I will send to you the Holy Spirit, the Comforter" (John 14:18).

Power. Voice. Comfort. Spirit. As you go about your activities this day, think about the Spirit. Remember: You've got it!

❖ When You Are Not Perfect

But as for me, I walk in my integrity; redeem me, and be gracious to me. My foot stands on level ground; in the great congregation I will bless the LORD. (Psalm 26:11-12)

Read Psalm 26.

The author of Psalm 26 is someone whom you would *not* want for a roommate. This is someone whom your mother might pick for your roommate, but even your mother wouldn't want to live next door to this person. Listen to him pray.

> I have walked in my integrity,
> and I have trusted in the LORD without
>   wavering. . . .
> I walk in faithfulness to you.
>
> I do not sit with the worthless,
>   nor do I consort with hypocrites;
> I hate the company of evildoers,
>   and will not sit with the wicked.
>
> I wash my hands in innocence, . . .
> But as for me, I walk in my integrity;
>   redeem me, and be gracious to me.
>   (Psalm 26:1, 3-6, 11)

It is said that Mark Twain spoke of someone as "a good man in the very worst sense of the word." Here he is! The author of Psalm 26. "God, I thank thee that I am so good. I have not wavered, have not sat with false people, evildoers, dissemblers, drug users, heavy drinkers, adulterers, blasphemers, sodomizers, fornicators, or other people who do those things described in the Bible with big words that are beyond our understanding but that sound bad."

Here is cool, calm, collected religion. It is religion of the covenant. "I will be your God, you will be my people." Obey my laws; all will go well for you. I have obeyed your law; all will go well with me. His prayer is thus an inventory of his virtues, a reminder of how well he has kept up his side of the bargain. Trust? Check. Faithfulness? Check. Innocence? Check.

He doesn't ask anything of God; for what is there to ask? His relationship to God is fixed, settled, complete, finished. This is the prayer of an obedient person who lives confidently in the structure. It is the prayer of the older brother who always stayed home and did what Mother told him to do; not the prayer of the younger prodigal son who had a taste for harlots and loose living (Luke 15).

According to this kind of religion, your job is to be obedient, to keep your hands clean, and not to press God too much about things. God's job is to respond when you push the right obedience button. Yet, if you push this sort of thing too far, you are on your way to an autonomous believer who really doesn't engage a transcendent partner. God really isn't needed by one with clean hands.

Count the times that "I," "me," "my" is used in Psalm 26: "*I* have walked," "*I* have trusted," "*my* heart and mind," "*my* eyes," "*I* walk," "*I* do not sit," "nor do *I* consort," "*I* hate," "*I* wash my hands," "*I* love," "*my* life," "*I* walk," "redeem *me*," "*I* will bless."

The result of this dull, frozen, religion of the "I" and the "me" and the "my" is the dissolution of the divine-human relationship. There is no surprise in the relationship anymore, nothing to amaze or confuse.

Psalm 26 is the prayer of the successful and the right. It is the prayer of the one for whom things have worked out right. I wanted to be team leader and I worked for it, and I got it. I wanted to get into college and I studied, and I got in. I wanted her or him for my spouse, and I succeeded. I wanted the job. I showed them my transcript, and I got it. And all will go well for you, as long as you stay right, and the sun shines, and your hands are clean. You can pray Psalm 26, groom your virtues, and get along quite nicely with yourself, without God. You don't need God for that.

Early in my ministry, I became acquainted with a young man who was active in a religious group on his campus. He always had the right Scripture verse on the tip of his tongue to cover every situation. He was the epitome of the wholesome, All-American boy. But one Christmas he came home for the holidays, and I thought that I noted a change in him. He seemed less self-assured, less confident that he always knew the right answer. I told him that I thought I had observed a change in him, a change that made him seem more accessible, more human. He confessed that he had committed a sin for which he felt great remorse. He said he was shocked that he, a "born-again Christian," could be capable of such sin. Then I knew why I liked him now: He was a real person rather than a stilted facade. His religion was now a way of dealing with the difficulties and failings of life rather than a means of suppressing and denying them. He could no longer pray Psalm 26 with a straight face. But there were lots better, lots deeper Psalms that he could now pray.

Carl Jung, a Swiss psychotherapist, noted that each of us wears a mask, a "persona," similar to the masks that were worn in ancient Greek drama. This is the face we present to others. It covers our "shadow," our true inner nature that we regard as unacceptable, unmentionable. Jung felt that the brighter and cleaner the persona, the darker the shadow underneath. My hands are clean. My life is right. My world is together.

Sometime after graduation he appeared in my office. He had been suffering from depression he said. He had even required hospitalization on one occasion. Because of his bouts with depression, it had been difficult for him to apply for jobs. Yet his psychiatrist said that he was making progress.

"It's funny," he said, "when I came here as a freshman, I was self-confident, self-assured. But now, I don't know what I believe. I feel insecure, unsure. Funny, I was more confident and knew more when I was a senior in high school than I do now that I'm a college graduate."

I said, "Look, I can explain that to you quickly. When you were eighteen you were more self-confident, more self-assured, because you were ignorant. Everybody feels right at eighteen. But now, with an education, you know what you don't know. You know that you are needy, vulnerable, weak. You know that you need others to help you get by. You've learned that you're not autonomous, not self-sufficient. Rejoice! You're a fast learner! Some people don't learn what you've learned until they are 45 and have had their first heart attack. You really did get an education here."

We can only come to God as we are—as sinful, frail, ordinary people. Fortunately, God takes us as we are. Your hands don't need to be spotless to be loved by this God.

Come as you are.

❖ Knowing Too Much for Your Own Good

They heard the sound of the LORD God walking in the garden at the time of the evening breeze, and the man and his wife hid themselves from the presence of the LORD God among the trees of the garden. But the LORD God called to the man, and said to him, "Where are you?" He said, "I heard the sound of you in the garden, and I was afraid, because I was naked; and I hid myself." (Genesis 3:8-10)

Read Genesis 3:1-19; Psalm 90.

It's a primitive story, primordial, which means basic, deep; a true story. It's from Genesis, the beginning of the Bible, the beginning of humanity. Genesis means "in the beginning." In the beginning, God made man and woman and put them in the garden. God will keep the good garden. All man and woman must do is to enjoy, to "be fruitful and multiply"—which sounds enjoyable.

It's a story like the ones told to and by children—naive, fairytale-like, deep, true—like the fairytales told to you when you were young.

Once upon a time, we had it all—with no business more pressing than "to be fruitful and multiply." Once upon a time we were like children, naked but unashamed, trusting, and unafraid. We were like a two-year-old after his bath, romping gleefully naked through the living room, free of the unnatural restraint called clothing. Undiapered and unashamed. The unselfconscious, trusting simplicity of children is the way God created us, so the story says, once upon a time.

Contra Augustine, this story is not an explanation of how sin came into the world. The story does not say the man and the woman were at one time sinless. It just says they were naked and unashamed like children—they were only a few days old, remember. It is a story, not about sin, but about *self-consciousness*. And because it's a story about human life, it's a story about *limits*.

You are free to enjoy the garden—only stay off that tree over there. The story does not ask, "Why that tree?" We're only told it's the "tree of the knowledge of good and evil." Therefore it's a tree of limits, for what makes us different from God is that we don't always know what is good, whereas God does. Because we're not God, we live with limits. Life has its limits. The story doesn't say why or how. It just states what everybody eventually learns after high school—life, as good as it often is, has limits. First, we don't know everything. Second, we shall die. The story depicts our first human testing, our pushing at the limits. It's not a story about Satan. This creature is a "snake" who, in the first days of development, was smarter than man or woman. (After all, we were only a few days old!) Like most smart beings, the snake was good at raising questions.

"Are you sure that God said . . . ?" "Why would God create such a fine tree and not allow you to eat?" (Socrates said that the purpose of a good teacher is to raise the right questions—just like the snake!) So we begin to wonder if life's limits apply to everyone else but us. Could a good God really say that we shall die?

Herein is our human dilemma. God has created us, male and female, the highest of animals. We have a won-

41

derfully contoured cerebral cortex. Since Genesis, we have bypassed snakes. We can reason, ask why, all on our own now, with no need of help from snakes. We can create, achieve, and discover. With all that we know, can it be that there is something which we cannot or should not know?

"Did God say there are *limits* to life in the Garden?" Surely not. Limits? Ah, that's the talk of primitive people, before science, in the time B.C.—before computers.

The man and woman, these wonders of creation, have been given the Garden. But they are also given boundaries. They are human, but also creatures. Being creatures, they cannot know all things, and they shall die. But having freedom, blessed with natural curiosity, they begin to push against the limits. "Did God say you shall not eat the fruit of *any* of the trees?" asks the snake, grossly misrepresenting what God said.

The woman corrects the snake. "No, God said we are free to use all the trees, except for one." But the thought has been planted.

"You will not die," says the serpent, moving from suggestion to outright rebellion. And why should we? It's not fair! So we take matters in hand.

We were told that we were creatures destined to enjoy the Creator; that, as creatures, all we must do is trust. But *we wanted knowledge more than trust.* We were told to entrust to God the meaning and significance of our lives, to let the Creator determine our destiny and worth as creatures. But that wasn't good enough. What good is a garden if we shall die? Not content to be creatures, we became creators. Look at what we can do and know if we just put our heads together! Go ahead, "a *little* knowledge is a dangerous thing." Eat up! Get wise.

Now, it's the Creator's turn to question. "Where are you?" And the creature gives a pitiful answer. "I was afraid. I was naked. I hid." We wanted knowledge rather than trust, and look what we got—a forlorn creature, shivering in the bushes, cringing in terror. We wanted to step over the boundaries, stand up and be free, and for all of this, we now know only one thing—namely, *we are naked.*

Our nakedness is no more apparent than in our pitiful attempts at self-justification through blaming. When asked "What have you done?" the woman says, "The serpent beguiled me." The man says, "The woman gave me. . . . " We can't admit our actions. It takes secure beings to be honest. The lying and blaming reveal the real truth about us: I was naked and afraid.

In the birth of human self-consciousness and rebellion, man and woman are punished—not by God, but by the results of their attempt to secure their lives by themselves rather than through trust in God.

"You will be in terrible pain in childbirth," the woman is told. "You will have desire for your husband, and he shall dominate you." This isn't God's will. God's will was for two companions in the Garden, being fruitful and multiplying. Now, relations between men and women are confused, a matter of power plays, dirty tricks, domination, submission. Even the joy of children will cause much pain.

To the man: "You shall be at war with the earth. It shall bring forth as many thorns as fruit. You shall sweat and labor over the dusty earth your whole life and then return to it in your death." The dry, rocky, inhospitable land of the Near East stood in contrast to the once friendly world of the Garden.

Now, in this topsy-turvy world out of joint, men and women are at odds with one another, and there is no joy that is not mixed with much pain, and we die. We are naked now, more than ever, lonely, nothing to secure us against the onslaughts of mortality. In the place of trust, we wanted knowledge. And look what we got.

You who are young may feel quite vulnerable and

afraid. You have lost enough of your innocence to know that there's a world of things out there you don't know. That relations between men and women are terribly conflicted.

You assume that your sense of vulnerability is a temporary by-product of being a young adult just out of high school, that someday it will be possible for you, perhaps in college, to acquire enough knowledge to overcome adolescent anxieties. By graduation, if all goes well, we will have succeeded in deceiving some of you into thinking that this has actually happened to you—that is, "I'm all grown up now and can at least take hold of my life and stand on my own two feet because I got an A in organic chemistry" (the closest one can come, before the senior year, to being as wise as Solomon).

And yet someday, if you live long enough, you may come to see that this was a great deceit; that, in truth, you are not strong, wise, and self-sufficient but really quite small, finite, mortal—namely, *naked and afraid*. You will be sitting in your den, dressed smartly in designer clothes, a large house surrounding you, but you will be naked. Your heart will skip a beat, there will be this strange sensation in your chest and you will smell mortality. Then you will see yourself located, not in some restricted Garden of Eden called "Westmont Estates," but in a weedy place where you are at enmity with the world, with other people, with life itself. And if asked "Why?," you may blame your situation on your parents, an inadequate exercise program, a lousy doctor, or your last spouse. Or you will say, if you muster as much honesty as Grandfather Adam, "I was naked . . . I was afraid."

Our attempt to know more is our effort to deal with our anxiety by circumventing the reality called God. If we can just know enough, build bigger and better systems of gaining knowledge, we can secure ourselves, carve out some enduring significance for ourselves.

The story, this old story, teaches otherwise. It is only

God who creates, permits, and prohibits; and it is only God who can deal with our deepest anxiety.

It's a hard lesson for us to learn. We who have been told that our greatest need is for autonomy, liberation and freedom, are not likely to heed the call to *trust*. Most of the sermons you've heard are calls to action, to use your potential, to achieve, live up to your great talent. This story suggests that this way is the *problem*, not the *solution*. The story says that any exercise of our potential that is not an admission of our boundaries is demonic because it is based on a lie.

It is a story, not about Adam and Eve, but about us because each of *us*, in our own lives, recapitulates this pri- mordial act of rebellion and self-deceit. The story there- fore has the power to shock us into recognition that our lives have enduring significance, not because we have learned so much, but because we learn to trust "in him we live and move and have our being" (Acts 17:28).

Which brings us to the end of the story. The story ends, not with this curse of pain and enmity of thorns and dusty death. It ends by saying that the Lord God, the Cre- ator, the Gardener, the Accuser, becomes the *Tailor*. God made, for the two creatures, *clothes*.

Creatures who know that they are naked need clothes, some protective covering as they go out into a now diffi- cult and bewildering world. God gives them what they need. God will not abandon them to their destructive delusions of self-sufficiency. God promised to punish them by death. But God's grace wins out, as it will many times again in our story. God refuses to give up on these two naked, frail, earthlings. God gives them clothes, and thus promises to continue to care for them, even in their silly presumption.

So, finite, frail, naked we are—yes, says the story. But also *loved*, preserved to live another day, clothed, fed, pro- tected, in order to know not just the facts of life and death, good and evil—but also *trust*.

❖ What Should You Do with Your Life?

And when Jesus had been baptized, just as he came up from the water, suddenly the heavens were opened to him and he saw the Spirit of God descending like a dove and alighting on him. And a voice from heaven said, "This is my Son, the Beloved, with whom I am well pleased." (Matthew 3:16-17)

As a pastor on a university campus, I spend a good deal of time with people who are trying to figure out who they are and what they ought to be doing. For 90 percent of the questioners, the *real* question is, Who am I?

One day, the door to my office swung open and a student entered. I looked up from whatever I was doing, startled by him. Without a word of introduction or explanation, he plopped down in one of my wing chairs and asked, "How did you know that you were supposed to be a preacher? Did you hear some voice from the sky? Did you always want to be a preacher? Did you ever think that you should do something else? How did you know?"

I responded, "Who sent you here? Who wants to know?"

Of course, *he* wanted to know, not so much because he was interested in me, in my call, but because he wanted to know something about himself. "Do you know a God who calls? If so, tell me about that because I've never heard God calling. Is it that some people hear from God and others don't?"

Perhaps we envy Jesus at his baptism. How easy it would be if the sky opened for us, the Holy Spirit came like a dove, a voice spoke, "This is my beloved Child, with whom I am well pleased."

We wouldn't need preachers with wing chairs, or

46

career counseling services, or Bible study groups if we were called as Jesus was. Of course, sometimes God does tell people who they are with dramatic, unambiguous experiences like the one at Jesus' baptism. I've talked to people who have had such experiences. It was as if a voice spoke to them, as if the veil of heaven was pulled back and they heard, they knew, they saw.

Most of us must be content with a revelation that is so ambiguous, veiled, and quiet that we often miss it if we're not careful. That's the way God speaks to most of us, not through some dove descended from heaven, but through some still small voice.

Dramatic, explicit visions of God are comparatively rare. Perhaps they are rare because we have become dull to the divine. Sometimes we only see what we dare to look for—and not everybody is looking or listening for God. But perhaps dramatic visions are rare because God's call is usually mediated, transmitted through people, a book, or an event. It slips in the back door.

The story of the dove descending at Jesus' baptism is thrilling and curious because it is so unusual. And the thing that strikes me, after a couple of decades of listening to people who are trying to listen to God, is how usual, how mundane, mediated, and ordinary is the sound of God's voice. From what I observe, there's usually no voice from above; there's a voice from within. The voice speaks so clearly that you know you heard it, yet it speaks so ambiguously that there are dozens of ways to explain it as something other than the voice of God; so you must respond to the voice on faith rather than complete certainty.

When I was in seminary, I remember the evening when one of our professors, James Dittes, shared with us the results of a decade of research into the personality characteristics of people who become pastors. Dittes devised a portrait called the "little adult" to describe the typical seminarian. The "little adult" was the child who was always more adult than child, one who got along well with authority figures, the boy or girl who was the school patrol guard, the classroom monitor when the teacher left the room. In other words, the "little adult" was the child who enforced adult values on other wayward children. Dittes theorized that such a child might be attracted to the ministry because, as a preacher, he or she could still enforce the values of the biggest adult (God) upon all the wayward adults.

On hearing this, one of my fellow seminarians blurted out, "This is terrible. You have just described me! As a child, I fit that description. Are you telling me that I am planning to be a minister out of my response to other people? Out of my own personality needs? I thought that I was here because God called me."

The professor replied, in some amazement, "Has God stopped calling people through other people?"

In the classes I teach, I ask seminarians, "How did you get here?" I've got people who have forsaken their parents' wishes for their lives, middle-aged computer programmers who walked off their good paying jobs and went to seminary, and other people who have heard that voice from within and have responded. And the thing that invariably impresses me, as I listen to their stories of vocation, is how utterly ordinary, unspectacular, and mundane was the voice they heard. They tell stories of people coming up to them after church and telling them they ought to think about being a preacher. They speak of books they read, a remark by a professor in the middle of a history class, a grandmother. Mundane, ordinary, unspectacular sources.

God's call, the divine response to the question "Who am I?" usually doesn't fall from heaven. So we have to listen. If I were to ask you today, "Who are you? How did you get here?" I expect that you would explain your presence at this stage of faith by reference to something or someone ordinary, commonplace, mundane.

I am not talking about "call," about "vocation," as if it

were something that only happens to preachers, only belongs to clergy. At our baptism, each of us is called to be a disciple, to try to do God's will, to search after God's desire for our lives. *All* Christians share that call to minister. Who am I? I am a disciple of Jesus, called to minister in his name. That some disciples are called to be pastors or priests doesn't change the call of every Christian, each in his or her own place, to be a minister of Jesus.

It usually takes time for you to hear your name being called. The claim of God upon your life must grow and ripen. In the story about the call of the young Samuel, Samuel's name was called three times. Elsewhere, God says, "Moses, Moses." When Paul is called on the Damascus Road, the voice says, "Saul, Saul." It's as if your name has to be called more than once for you gradually to catch on that this is God dealing with *you*. That this is *God* dealing with you.

And, when God is calling you, God will use any handle God can get. Don't be surprised if you feel that God is speaking to you in the middle of some crisis in your life, just when you feel most confused, least sure of what you ought to do. God will use any handle God can get.

A good rule of thumb, when thinking about what you ought to do with your life, what God wants you to do, who God wants you to be is this: *Where the great needs of the world intersect with your God-given gifts—that is your call. And God will use any handle God can get.*

❖ Be Who You Are

> Owe no one anything, except to love one another; for the one who loves another has fulfilled the law. The commandments, "You shall not commit adultery; You shall not murder; You shall not steal; You shall not covet"; and any other commandment, are summed up in this word, "Love your neighbor as yourself."
> (Romans 13:8-9)

49

Read Romans 12:2, 9-20.

In Shakespeare's *Hamlet,* there is the scene where old Polonius—an aging, sentimental blowhard—gives advice to his son, Laertes. Laertes is preparing to leave for France and old Polonius, knowing what sometimes happens to eighteen year olds in Paris, does what fathers do—he offers advice.

Polonius' speech to his son is a great favorite of Shakespeare lovers. My high school English teacher read it to us the last day of class our senior year. I even found it painted in six foot letters on the walls of the dining hall at the University of Indiana for all the students to meditate upon as they chewed breakfast. As it turns out, Polonius' advice, like a lot of advice fathers give their sons, is mostly hot air and doesn't bear much analysis:

> "Be thou familiar, but by no means vulgar. . . .
> Give every man thy ear, but few thy voice. . . .
> Neither a borrower, nor a lender be. . . .
> This above all: to thine own self be true,
> And it must follow, as the night the day,
> Thou canst not then be false to any man." (Act I,
> Sc. III)

What is that supposed to mean? "To thine own self be true?" Act like *yourself?* Most parents hope that's the last thing their sons or daughters will do when they leave home! They would rather they act as the parents wish they would. Laertes, like most eighteen year olds, politely stands on one foot and then the other while his old man prattles about, "Neither a borrower nor a lender be; . . . to thine own self be true." After all, parental advice doesn't usually do harm—as long as it's not taken *too* seriously. Can you imagine some of the things your parents have told you printed in six foot letters across the wall of university cafeteria? *"Pick up your socks or you'll never get married!"*

No wonder most people have become inoculated to

advice by the time they reach your age. It's the self-protective mechanism of the young to preserve themselves from the onslaughts of the Poloniuses of the world.

Generally my advice to people your age is, "Don't listen to advice." I say that, not only because that is something with which you would agree, but also because questionable advice like, "Don't sweat Organic Chemistry," is always so much more appealing than really sound advice like, "Worry about everything."

If you are skeptical of *my* advice, perhaps you will take the advice of Paul in Romans 12–13.

It all sounds like something your mother might tell you, doesn't it? Here is Paul giving advice, a list of do's and don'ts. And I suppose that this sort of thing is what most people think religion is all about. Don't do this. Don't do that. Polonius giving advice to Laertes; Paul advising the church at Rome.

For the first eleven chapters of Paul's Letter to the Romans, he speaks of the unmerited, utterly free, gracious love of God. "There is therefore now no condemnation for those who are in Christ" (8:1). "God shows his love for us in that while we were yet sinners Christ died for us" (5:1). God's love is for the righteous and the unrighteous, Jew and Gentile, because "God shows no partiality" (2:1). But at last Paul reveals his true colors. He's preached grace, acceptance, love, forgiveness long enough. Now's the time to get down to what he really wanted to tell us: Advice. A long list of do's and don'ts. Enough of this grace business.

In preparing my advice to you, based upon Paul's advice to the Romans, I discovered something. As we read in the Bible, Paul tells them, "Let love be genuine; hate what is evil, hold fast to what is good; love one another." But that isn't what Paul said. In the Greek, the verb is in the imperative rather than the indicative. It's not, "Let love be genuine; hate this, hold to this, do that." It's, "Love is genuine. It hates evil, clings to what is good." The verb is indicative, not imperative.

Despite the tone, Paul isn't saying, Do this. Don't do that. He is saying, *be this.* For eleven chapters of this epistle Paul has used every means at his disposal—argument, narrative, hymn, poem, reason, humor—to tell the Romans that in Jesus Christ they are royalty. They are the first witnesses to a new age, the first citizens of a new kingdom. Then, at the beginning of chapter twelve, comes the Greek word *oun,* meaning *therefore.* Therefore, be not conformed to this world (because you are of a new world). Therefore, serve the Lord (because you have been served by the Lord). Therefore, practice hospitality (because God has been hospitable to you, a stranger). Therefore, bless those who persecute you (because Jesus blessed you, even when you crucified him).

See what Paul is doing here? It's ethics. But not ethics like we usually do ethics. Here is an ethic based not upon moralizing lists of do's and don'ts, the shrill, carping advice of the ethically presumptuous. Here is an ethic based upon who we really are and are meant to be.

There are two ways to go at this matter of advice, you see. One way is for your mother to sit you down and say, "Now, you're going off to college. College is a big, strange place, so you be careful. Don't you let me hear of you not doing your best. You must study hard, get the grades, hit the books." Do this, do that.

Another way is for your mother to sit you down and tell you how proud she is of all that you are as a person of gifts, of sensitivity, and of goodness. *Be who you are.*

My sister recalls leaving home for some Saturday night adventure and hearing our mother bidding her farewell with, "Remember, you *are* somebody." That's what Paul wanted to say to you. "Don't be conformed." You don't need to be. You *are* somebody.

So many times we think of ethics as a matter of answering, What ought I to do? In the matter of abortion, or sexual behavior, cheating, or truthfulness, What ought I to do? But how does one answer that question without the prior question, Who am I and who do I want to be? In Christian ethics, the indicative precedes the imperative. Who am I? comes before, What ought I to do?

Love is genuine. It hates what is evil, holds fast to what is good, blesses those who persecute, repays no one evil for evil. You are God's beloved, therefore . . .

Be who you are, says Paul—namely, those who are in Christ. Structure your life and deal with others as God has dealt with you.

❖ Forgiving as Remembering

Do not remember the sins of my youth or my trans-gressions; according to your steadfast love remember me, for your goodness' sake, O LORD! (Psalm 25:7)

Read Psalm 25.

"Remember not the sins of my youth." What an evocative phrase. What are these "sins of youth" for which the psalmist begs divine amnesia?

Sins of my youth! I see smoke-filled, sleazy dives known as "Sam's Bar and Grill." I think of all night binges, by a person about the age of a college sophomore, followed by aching head or Saint Augustine, who spent the rest of his life repaying God for debts incurred during youthful degradation, praying, "O Lord, make me chaste, but not yet!" For this prayer he was named patron saint of all wayward students. Sins of youth!

Every person over ten or twelve has some secret room somewhere, a trunk hidden away in the attic, or a closed casket buried deep in the basement of the soul cluttered with dark moments and memories we would just as soon forget. And the older you get the more memory you try to put in that room, that trunk, that grave; the older you grow, the more you have to forget. What is remorse but bitter memory? What is guilt but accusing memory?

The most frequent sort of suffering I encounter when counseling people is suffering brought on by memory. Where come this nervousness, sleeplessness, nailbiting, tossing and turning, and drug taking except from the feelings of fear, suspicion, anxiety resulting from memory too painful to bear? We fill our rooms with the trophies, diplomas, rings, photographs, and blue ribbons of good memories. But deeply hidden in the center of our being are the memories too painful to remember.

Our first response to undesirable memories is to try to forget them. "Let's agree to forget about it. Let's both act as if this just never happened."

"Why dwell on the past? What's done is done. Let's talk about something more pleasant."

Remember not the sins of my youth. But bad memory unremembered, pushed back into the secret place of ourselves, does much harm. The unconscious has no digestive tract. It's not as if we can just swallow hard and have our painful past leave our consciousness and be done with it. We've tried to do that as a nation with national traumas. We've tried to do it as individuals. When we try to forget the painful memories, we become strangers to ourselves because we cut down our history to pleasant, comfortable size—the stuff of our daydreams rather than our nightmares. Burying our past, says Henri Nouwen, is turning our back on our best teacher.

We wish our past were over and done with, but it's not done with us, not yet. We're not the escape artists we wish we were. We chatter, make jokes, turn on the radio, take a drink, try to live only for today. But then there's that face, the casual gesture, the wisp of an old tune, and we remember.

We wish to God that we could forget!

Remember not just the things we did on Saturday night, but also what we did all week: the way we treated our parents; the people, people whose names we can't even remember, whom we hurt in thought, word, and deed; the things done and left undone. Dare we remember even for a moment? We know the ancient, honest words of confession are right, *"We have followed too much the desires and devices of our own hearts. There is no health in us. We are not worthy to be called thy children."*

We wish to God that God could forget!

The wishing to forget is not over and done with when you're twenty-one. You've just begun to want to forget. If children must yearn for their parents' forgiveness and forgetfulness, how much more ought we parents to seek the forgiveness of our children. Someday every parent looks at his or her grown children and thinks not, "Look at all I have done for them," but "Look at all I have done *to* them." How can there ever be enough forgetfulness to go around?

A student said of his younger sister who was in her second year of psychotherapy for chemical dependence, "If she could only learn to forgive our parents for what they did or didn't do to her. If she could only learn to forgive herself for what she did or didn't do to them." Perhaps the therapist could help her to remember and then to forget.

If we yearn for the forgetfulness of other people, how much more ought we to beg for the forgetfulness of God. As another Psalm asks, "O Lord, if thou should count our iniquities, Lord, who could stand?" (Ps. 130:3 AP).

If God is omniscient, omnipresent, all knowing and all wise, think of the pain God must endure because of us. At least we are human. We are prone to let some things pass. Eventually, many of our wounds heal. Amnesia sets in, and we achieve relative peace. I can't even remember what I had for lunch yesterday, much less whom I offended. But God? If God remembers everything, God must suffer terribly. How can God endure the silence of the universe if God remembers, as vividly as if yesterday,

Hiroshima, Auschwitz, the Battle of Hastings, and last moment's unkind thought or deed of meanness?

Does God have the alleged memory of an elephant? "Smith? Is that E. Smith? Yes, let's see. Gabriel, bring me the file on E. Smith." Lord, who could stand?

The woman at the well said, "My husband," and Jesus, the one with divine memory, reminded her, "You've had five husbands, and the man you're living with now, as I recall, is not your husband." She ran to her friends crying, "Come see a man who told me everything I ever did."

So the psalmist cries, "Remember not the sins of my youth, or my transgressions." Forget it. We wish to God that God could forget.

Some day each of us stands before our father and mother, looks into their eyes, and sees reflected back our youth, the demands we made, the words we said, the ways we disappointed and hurt without even trying, and we silently ask for their forgiveness, their forgetfulness.

Some day, each of us will ask the same forgetfulness of God. Remember not. Will God forget?

One day Thomas Aquinas was lecturing to his students on the omnipotence of God. God is all-powerful, all-knowing. "Is there any way in which God is limited?" a student asked the learned Aquinas.

"Yes," he replied. A shocked hush fell upon the classroom. "Yes. Even God Almighty cannot make the past not to have been."

Even God Almighty cannot wipe out our past. What's done is done. What's done is remembered, and what's remembered, even the sins of our long past youth, is forever. We are trapped, desolate, doomed to bear the burden of our past forever.

I'll tell you who your real friends are: A friend is someone who knows you, remembers you perhaps better than you know yourself, *but who doesn't remember*. Friends are those who discreetly forget, before whom certain things don't have to be dredged up, recollected. For the sake of love, they forget. A friend is someone who forgets what you've *done* in order never to forget who you *are*.

Remember not the sins of my youth. Remember *me*. That's what each of us wants from God: That God will love us enough to forget what we have done and left undone, in thought, word, and deed, in order that God might remember us. In Scripture, such divine forgetfulness is called *forgiveness*. On our knees, with outstretched hands, that's the mercy for which we beg, the mercy that God will forget in order to remember. "Smith? Is that E. Smith? Forget the file. I remember you. I remember you."

Two Psalms later the poet recalls, "If my father or mother forsake me, LORD, you will take me" (27:10 AP).

"Remember not the sins of my youth, or my transgressions; according to thy steadfast love remember *me*!"

❖ Downward Mobility

Let the same mind be in you that was in Christ Jesus,
who, though he was in the form of God,
    did not regard equality with God
    as something to be exploited,
but emptied himself,
    taking the form of a slave,
    being born in human likeness.
And being found in human form,
    he humbled himself
    and became obedient to the point of death—
even death on a cross.

Therefore God also highly exalted him
    and gave him the name
    that is above every name,
so that at the name of Jesus
    every knee should bend,

in heaven and on earth and under the earth,
and every tongue should confess
that Jesus Christ is Lord,
to the glory of God the Father. (Philippians 2:5-11)

There are some passages of Scripture that can best be described as drama with a plot, a story, a beginning and end. Others are like a symphony, with adagio and crescendo.

Can you hear the movement in this scripture? "Though he was God, he emptied himself, and became obedient unto death, even death on a cross. Therefore God has highly exalted him and bestowed on him the name which is above every name." Feel the movement? Jesus was like God, up there, above everything. Yet, he came down, humbled himself, even as low as the most humbling experience of all, even unto death, even death on a cross. You don't get much higher than God. You don't get much lower than a cross. He began high. He ended low.

This movement, this emptying, is what Henri Nouwen has called "downward mobility." It is a Gospel dance. Philippians 2:6-11 is an early Christian hymn. You can actually hear embedded in this letter of Paul to the Philippians the beat, the movement. It begins high. It ends low. Downward mobility.

This is the movement, the dance, which Paul wants to fix in our brains. "Have this mind among yourselves," Paul says. Make this movement part of you.

A woman teaches high school history in a depressed, remote part of South Carolina. Her students have so little, and she tries so hard to teach them. One day, in frustration at their poor performance on an exam she puts down her head on her desk and just sobs. "I wish I could open up those thick heads of yours and pour this history in!" she cries.

Paul might say to her, "It's easier to teach history than to teach Christ." For the challenge is not simply to impart information *about* Jesus—there really isn't much information about Jesus in the Bible—but to teach *the very mind of Jesus*. Paul wants them not just to know the hymn, but to make this hymn so much a part of them that they hum it, tap their toes to it, can't get it out of their heads.

A college Department of Religion will teach you *about* religion. You can learn about Buddhism and Christianity. They make Christianity something that is academically acceptable—Christianity as sociology, the church as history, Jesus as a worthy subject for a Master's thesis. Religion courses teach you *about* Christianity, but dare they teach Christianity?

Nobody is changed, no one's mind is blown or rearranged, from studying *about* Christ. Paul says that church isn't Religion 101. Put your pencils and notebooks away. There is no textbook, no exam. Reading the Bible is an attempt to get the mind of Christ in your mind until his mind, his movement, becomes so much a part of you that it *is* you.

When you take ballroom dancing, you learn the "box step." There is a chart with two little black feet facing two little white feet that shows the steps: his right foot forward, her left foot back, then her right foot right, his left foot left. It's awkward at first. But by your second visit, you're doing it by the numbers and by your third formal dance, dancing cheek to cheek in the middle of the floor, it's part of you. You aren't counting, you aren't thinking, you're dancing. It's you.

An African tribe, before going on the hunt, gathers the hunters around the fire. Someone dresses up like a lion. The hunters dance with the lion. They thrust their spears toward the lion, they sing, they dance, they enact the hunt. Do you see what they're doing? They're learning the moves, going through the motions they will need tomorrow in the hunt, so that when they face a real lion, the movement of courage will be so much a part of them that they can do it without having to think about it. They've learned the moves.

You can't follow Christ without being *in* Christ. You can't know Jesus by knowing about Jesus. He's got to get in you. Your mind must be his mind. Learning Christ is much like learning to dance.

It isn't easy, for here is a strange move, much stranger than the box step. If it is odd for God to empty himself— to take the form of a servant, to wait on someone else's table, to wash someone else's wounds, to be rejected, to be slapped, to have someone else's spittle run down his cheeks, to be dressed up and mocked as a king, to be whipped and then nailed to the cross with criminals—it is even more odd for us.

Most people don't go to college to move down. Being in Christ is a difficult dance for you and me to learn, a tough procession with which to keep in step, a narrow way down, which ultimately leads us up. Will you try it?

❖ Don't Go Out There Alone

"Be strong in the Lord and in the strength of his power. Put on the whole armor of God, so that you may be able to stand." (Ephesians 6:10-11)

Read Ephesians 6:10-20.

This is not one of my favorite biblical texts; it may be one of yours. I have trouble with military metaphors as descriptions of the Christian life. "Be strong in the Lord. . . . Put on the whole armor of God. . . . Take the shield of faith . . . Take the helmet of salvation, and the sword of the Spirit." This mixing of the martial with the gospel is dangerous. Some of the darkest days of church history occurred when Christians marched out with banners unfurled to crusade, to make holy war. What do these military images have to do with the religion of the Prince of Peace? Is Ephesians 6:10-20 a worthy expression of the Christian faith?

When asked for their first association when hearing "Onward Christian Soldiers," a majority of respondents said, "The need for the church to be in mission throughout the world." When asked what they think about when they hear "The Battle Hymn of the Republic," they said, "The Civil Rights Movement of the 1960's and the fight for racial justice." Perhaps we forget, in a time of tame churches, toned-down preachers, and timid prophets that there was a time when the church believed that there was something worth fighting for.

What do you think about when you are urged to "Put on the whole armor of God . . . For our struggle is not against enemies of blood and flesh , but against the rulers, against authorities, against the cosmic powers of this present darkness . . . take the whole armor of God, . . . the breastplate of righteousness, . . . the shield of faith . . . the sword of the Spirit"?

Is there anything worth fighting for today? Is there anything in your world so inimicable to the way of Christ that you need some sword and shield to protect you?

The writer to the Ephesians wrote these words "in chains." He told his congregation, *If you plan to follow Jesus, get ready for a real fight.*

I wonder if this text from Ephesians 6, telling Christians to prepare for battle, means more to some of you than to me because of a difference between the generations. I was raised in a church where the main agenda of the church was to help Christians to adapt to the world as it is. Many of you have grown up in a church where the agenda is how to help you to survive as a Christian. (Please note that the armament listed in Ephesians 6 is mostly of a defensive nature—helmet, shield, breastplate—the armor needed for survival rather than attack.)

I was born into a world where Christians seemed secure, confident, and powerful, in the United States of the 1950s. My parents worried little about whether or not I would grow up Christian—it was the only game in town. The entire town was closed on Sundays. Everyone went to church. It was the American, accepted, normal thing to do. In that world the church did not have to bother itself too much about defensive maneuvers because, after all, we were fortunate to live in a basically Christian country. It was *our* world.

A few years ago I woke up and realized that, whether or not my parents were justified in believing this, we cannot believe it today. American Christians—conservative or liberal, Roman Catholic or Protestant—cannot believe anymore that our children will become Christian simply by drinking the water, and breathing the air. If our children grow into this faith, we will have to help them there. If we are to hold on to and live out this faith, we will have to do so with care and determination, because sometime between 1950 and 1970 the world shifted. It was no longer "natural" and "American" to be Christian.

Paganism, the worship of false gods, is the air we breathe, the water we drink. It captures us, it converts our young, it subverts our church. The writer of Ephesians did not have to be convinced that the world was a hostile, inhospitable place for discipleship. These words were written "in chains." That world recognized the subversive nature of the Christian faith and put Christians in chains. Our world recognizes the subversive nature of the Christian faith and subverts us by ignoring us. The world has declared war upon the gospel in the most subtle of ways, so subtle that sometimes you don't know you're losing the battle until it's too late.

In the oddest of ways, the gospel brings about a head-on collision with many of our culture's most widely held and deeply believed values. Being a Christian today is neither natural nor easy.

Thus the writer to the Ephesians says that you had better not go out unarmed. It is tough out there. The world lives by different slogans, different visions, speaks a different language than that of the church. So we must gather to "speak the truth in love" (4:15) so that we might grow up in our faith. Weak, childish, immature faith is no match for the world. Being a Christian is too difficult a way to walk alone.

Last year I was talking to a student who is a member of a dormitory Bible study group. He was telling me that he had never been in a Bible study group before, never felt the need of it back home. "Why here?" I asked. "Have you any idea how difficult it is to be a sophomore and a Christian at the same time?" he replied.

It's tough out there. Paganism is the air we breathe, the water we drink—and I'm not only talking about what they do in the dorms on Saturday nights—which is often quite pagan—but also what they do in the classrooms on Monday morning. You better not go out there alone, without comrades in arms, without your sword and your shield.

So we must gather, on a regular basis, for worship. We must speak about God in a world that lives as if there is no God. We must speak to one another as beloved brothers and sisters in a world that encourages us to live as strangers. We must pray to God to give us what we cannot have by our own efforts in a world that teaches us that we are self-sufficient and all powerful. In such a world, what we do on Sunday morning becomes a matter of life and death. Pray that I might speak the gospel boldly (Ephesians 6:20).

A couple of years ago, I was invited to preach in the congregation where a friend of mine serves. The congregation is located in the heart of one of our great cities. The congregation is made up entirely of people who live in the tenement houses in that part of the city. I arrived at eleven o'clock, expecting to participate in about an hour of worship. But I did not rise to preach until nearly half past twelve. There were five or six hymns and gospel songs, a great deal of speaking, hand-clapping, and singing. We did not have the Benediction until nearly quarter past one. I was exhausted.

"Why is the worship service in the black church so long?" I asked my friend as we went out to lunch. "Our worship never lasts much over an hour."

He smiled. Then he explained, "Unemployment runs nearly 50 percent here. For our youth, the unemployment rate is much higher. That means that, when our people go about during the week, everything they see, everything they hear tells them, 'You are a failure. You are nobody. You are nothing because you do not have a good job, you do not have a fine car, you have no money.'

"So I must gather them here, once a week, and get their heads straight. I get them together, here, in the church, and through the hymns, the prayers, the preaching say, 'That is a lie. You are somebody. You are royalty! God has bought you with a price and loves you as his Chosen People.' It takes me so long to get them straight because the world perverts them so terribly."

I hope that you will be in church this Sunday. I hope that church will help you get your head straight, gain the equipment you need, see the visions you deserve, learn to name the name that saves because it's tough out there.

❖ Jesus Has Been There

After three days they found him in the temple, sitting among the teachers, listening to them and asking them questions. And all who heard him were amazed. (Luke 2:46-47)

Read Luke 2:41-52.

Over the altar at Duke University Chapel on what's called the reredos, carved in limewood is an episode from Jesus' childhood. The boy Jesus before the elders in the Temple.

I've traveled much, visited many churches, studied art history. I know of no other church in the world which has that not-too-well-known scene from Jesus' life in so prominent a place. I know of no inconographic parallels in churches either ancient or modern. There, as center-piece of the scuptural program of our Chapel, stands little Jesus before the big, adult scholars of the Temple.

We know nothing of Jesus' childhood except for this one episode. As a boy, did Jesus help Joseph in his carpenter's shop? We don't know. Did he sometimes accompany his mother, Mary, on her trips to market? We don't know. The only thing we know of him as a boy was that he aston-ished the scholars at the Temple with this knowledge of the Bible. He dared to debate them, dared to interpret scripture to the interpreters. He looks to be about twelve on the reredos. There Jesus is. And there are the scholars. You can clearly see on their faces the amazement.

As you are leaving one school and entering another, I want you to ponder this: We don't know anything about Jesus from his birth in Bethlehem until he's an adult except for this—he was a spectacular student; he amazed the teachers, knew more about the Bible than men who had spent their whole lives studying scripture. Why is this all that we know about Jesus from birth until about age 30? Why, of all the scenes from his life, was this deemed to be among the most important for portrayal at Duke Chapel?

Here's what I think. I think that scene of Jesus before the scholars at the Temple was put in a university chapel for everyone who's young enough, small enough, to remember what it's like to be in school.

I'm old, grown up, beyond the reach of formal educa-tion, but I can still remember a little about school. For one thing, I remember the smell. Schools smell like—schools. They have a special odor. Not a bad odor exactly. It's just an odor like—school. Another thing. Schools don't have telephones. In every school I've ever been in, there's only one telephone. It's in the office. It's guarded by this person, the same one who guards the permission slips and the staplers. Even if you're a teacher, you have to go through this guard to use the telephone. For some reason schools believe that, if you have a telephone sitting out in the open where some geometry teacher might try to use it without permission, the whole place would explode into anarchy. Once they get you in school, they don't want you trying to make contact with the real world.

When you're all grown up, it's hard to remember what it's like to be in school. Hard to remember, that is, until you leave a little one at the door and drive away, or go to a parents' conference and you're told by the teacher why your child is not doing well in algebra; and then you say, "Now I remember how much I hated algebra when I was in school and why I had to become anything other than an accountant when I grew up."

I had forgotten what it was like to be in school, what it was *really* like, until a few years ago when I went back to school. I decided to brush up on my German. I started in first-year German. Eight freshmen and me. I had forgotten what it was like to be in school.

"Please tell us the prepositions that require the accusative."

"Well, let's see. There is *an, auf,* or is it *aus, ausser*?"

"We are waiting. Prepositions that require the accusative. Surely you know them. You had all weekend to prepare."

"But I was rather busy this weekend and . . ."

"We do not want to have to hurt you."

"Oh yes, *aus, ausser, bei, mit, nach, seit, von, zu.*"

It was homecoming weekend. At the end of class on Friday, the professor said, "By the way, class, I will give

66

you a quiz on Monday. Last six chapters." She brushed out the door.

"Are you people going to take that?" I asked the class (after the professor had left). "Don't you people have any plans for the weekend? I do. Tell her we don't want a quiz on Monday."

"*You* tell her," they said.

It was a busy weekend.

I had forgotten, you see, what it is like to be in school— that is to say, *What it was like to be small.* School has a way of making you the smallest you will ever be in your whole life.

In my freshman seminar last year there was a person who sat through most of the semester and never opened her mouth in class discussion. One night, she at last made a comment so succinct, so right, so to the point—and she made it in a marvelously melodically accented voice (similar to my own). After class I pulled her aside.

"I ought to wring your neck. Why didn't you speak up in class before now? You have a lot to say. We need you."

"Well, I'm from a tiny high school in a little town in South Carolina and all these people know so much and have been so many places. I was scared to speak."

"I'm from a little town in South Carolina," I said, "and look at me."

But you see, she was a student. She was still in school. You know what that's like. *Small.* Vulnerable. Not wishing to appear stupid. There are few things more horrible than the derisive, scornful laughter of a classroom, particularly when the laughter is led by the teacher. And I have been known to wake up in a cold sweat at night having dreamed that I was back in high school and I was staring at a black— abysmally black—board, class to my back, chalk in hand, having been sent there to conjugate a Latin verb.

A little boy was sent home one day with a note pinned to his coat reading, "Thomas is too dumb to learn. School is a waste for him." His name was Thomas Alva Edison.

School can make you feel the smallest you will ever feel in life.

A little boy from a poor, uneducated family stands before the scholars in the temple, toe-to-toe with them, instructing rather than being instructed by them. The story is childlike, a kind of fairytale right at the beginning of Jesus' life. It belongs with other such stories, told and retold by children. Jack outsmarts the giant. Little Red Riding Hood puts one over on the wolf. Little David gets the best of great big Goliath.

It's a childlike snapshot of the boy Jesus. Uncomplicated, playful, easy to remember. It is a story told with delight by little people, those who do not do well on the SAT, those who do not have access to powerful thoughts and big ideas. It is a story to be told again and again by those who can't get to the great books of the Western world, who don't even try to fill out the admissions application because they cannot endure another rejection, people who when you say "University" hear about a place they will never go, who when they hear "school" get a sick feeling in the stomach.

For whom was this story told? Who among us then or now would have heard it and exclaimed, "You tell 'em, Jesus!"

I believe it was told for the little people. This is the sort of story that electrifies the small, the weak, the vulnerable by reminding them whose side God is on, who God's advent means to astonish. Mother Mary had sung, when told she would have a baby, "God is going to bring down the proud and lift up the lowly." We see that in this story, live, before our eyes.

It is a story meant to unnerve the scholars, to make uneasy those who know the Bible backwards and forwards, who always have just the right chapter and verse on the tip of the tongue. It means to create a new world where deliverance is at hand for those who are small, and those on the bottom get to go to the head of the class, and little Jesus knows more than people with a Ph.D.

So in a way, it's everybody's story, this story of little Jesus astounding the big people at the Temple, because in a funny way, *everybody gets to be small someday.* I wish I could tell you who are young that the bigger you get, the more grown up you become, the more certain you are of the right answers. But no matter how big and adult you get, there are still times when you feel small. It might be in school, in a hospital, or in a family. Everybody gets to be small, someday.

And this story says, *Jesus has been there.* He knows what it's like. Luke says that, after amazing these scholars at the Temple, Jesus obediently returned home with his parents, back home to where he "increased in wisdom and stature"—which is a fancy way of saying he grew up. But little Jesus never got so big that he couldn't remember what it was like to stand before the educational, intellectual, theological powers and be made to answer. He never got so educated, tamed, and refined that he got over his youthful tendency to stand before the educational, political, economic powers as a kid and to ask them tough questions.

Later in Luke, Jesus says, "They will hand you before Kings and into law courts, they will test you, quiz you, force you to answer. Don't be afraid! The Holy Spirit will tell you what to say. I'll give you the answer you need. *I've been there.*"

❖ Flunking the Only Exam That Matters

Then some of the scribes answered, "Teacher, you have spoken well." For they no longer dared to ask him another question. (Luke 20:39-40)

69

Read Luke 20:19-47.

Have you ever dreamed that you were in school taking an exam? It's a fairly typical dream of alumni. The dream often involves some problem you have with the exam. You have studied all night for the final in organic chemistry. But now, on the morning of the exam, you find that the classroom door is locked. You pound on the door, but you can't get in. Another such dream involves your sauntering into class one day and discovering to your horror that it's the day of the exam but for some reason, you never got the word. Then you awake in a cold sweat, trembling all over, only to find that it's a dream. You breathe a sigh of relief; you have graduated. No more exams! As a student, don't you long for the day when exams will be only the stuff of bad dreams after an evening of Mexican food?

I believe exam nightmares are testimony to our residual bad memories of what it was like, as a student, to be under faculty assault. Exam time is a time to "show your stuff," to "lay it on the line." Can you pass the test?

It's no fun to stay up half the night only to receive for your efforts a paper filled with blood-red marks, to look like a fool in front of the whole class, to find your name on the professor's door at the very bottom of the grade list. Exams.

And sometimes I wonder if that's the purpose of exams, to keep you vulnerable, small, threatened. Oh, we say it's to measure how much history or chemistry you have inhaled, but I wonder if some exams have as their purpose to convince you that you did not learn all that much in the course; that though you thought you mastered German, there is still more that you don't know than you know; that you may never know enough to be as smart as your professor.

Exams do more than measure knowledge. They are also useful for keeping certain people locked out of the room of success, for keeping some people in a sweat.

During the final week of his earthly life, as he moved toward his cross, Jesus was put to the test. Luke 20 tells of Jesus' exam, Jesus' final exam, a three-part test consisting of three essay questions put to Jesus by his critics. Tension has been steadily building throughout Luke's Gospel. Now, Jesus' enemies have at last gathered enough strength to test him. Here is a three-question exam bigger for Jesus than the SATs; for here is an exam, not in Religion 101, but in life. If Jesus flunks this, he's lost all; *he's dead*. This isn't a matter of being shut out of med school; it's a matter of life or death.

"Then the Pharisees went and took counsel how to entangle him in his talk." (Luke 20:15). The method of entanglement is a no-win sort of question.

Exam question 1. "Teacher, . . . you are true, and teach the way of God truthfully, and care for no human opinion . . . Tell us, then, . . . Is it lawful to pay taxes to Caesar, or not?" (vv. 21-22 AP)

It's a setup. If Jesus answers no, the Romans will label him a Jewish revolutionary and kill him. If he answers yes, the religious leaders will say he has defiled God, for to pay taxes to Caesar is to pay with the idolatrous coinage stamped with Caesar's pagan image—a crime for a faithful Jew.

Jesus, aware of their cunning deceit, answers their question with another. "Do you have a coin on you?" he asks. They produce a denarius. "Whose picture is on the coin?" he asks.

"Why, Caesar's," they say.

"Well, that settles it," says Jesus, giving them one of the greatest non-answers of all time. "Render to Caesar what's Caesar's, but give to God what is God's."

Behind this interchange there is an answer. They have one of Caesar's idolatrous coins on them; Jesus' pockets are empty. They are examining Jesus about his stance toward the Roman occupation forces in Judea while they collaborate with the Romans. They carry Caesar's coins—

which become silent but irrefutable proof of their own compromised faith.

A fresh team of examiners shows up—the Sadducees (Luke 20:27-40). Unlike the Pharisees, the Sadducees deny the resurrection of the dead (which Jesus has made central to his message); so, through exam question 2, the Sadducees hope to kill two birds—the Pharisees and Jesus—with one stone.

Question 2. A Nazarean rabbi believes in the resurrection of the dead. Now, a man dies, leaving a widow without children. In obedience to Levitical law, she marries his brother. But the brother dies without issue as well. So the two-time widow marries a third brother. He dies without issue. This one unfortunate bride works through a total of seven brothers and seven funerals. Whose wife will she be after the resurrection?

This one wasn't on the study sheet. It's a toughy. It makes belief in the resurrection seem dumb. The poor woman can't be married to all seven brothers at once. It doesn't seem right for her to be married only to one. What's the answer?

Jesus again throws the whole thing back in the face of his examiners. The resurrection isn't dumb, you're what's dumb. We're talking resurrection of the dead here, not just an extension of all the unjust, unequal, and dead social arrangements with which you are familiar where women are no more than the property of this man or that one. The resurrection is God's reworking of everything you've messed up. It's a whole, new, God-created ballgame to which your old rules don't apply!

Again Jesus questions them. "What do you think of the Christ? Who do *you* think is the Messiah?" He has asked them a question, *the* question. "Who is the Messiah? Who could deliver you?"

"No one was able to answer him a word," says Luke. "For they no longer dared to ask him any question." In case you're keeping score, the score is: Jesus-3, authorities-0.

Then, fed up with his Mickey Mouse version of the "$64,000 Question," Jesus blows his top and lets them have it. He tells the professor what he thinks of their religious SAT! I'm sorry that those of you who think Jesus was a nice guy have to hear this, but Jesus tears into them, *ad hominem*, calling them every dirty name he can think of—hypocrites, child of hell, blind guides, extortioners, whitewashed tombs, brood of vipers (Matt. 23:1-36). It is the maddest, meanest, angriest Jesus that anybody has ever seen.

Why is Jesus so mad? You may wonder. You've had professors who were unfair on exams. You may have socked it to one teacher on a course evaluation form, but here Jesus burns down the professor's office! Why is he at last so angry?

I don't know. But perhaps Jesus has had enough of examinations. He knows what they're after with their questions.

Jesus came to us, offering us life, and we gave him— questions. Elsewhere people asked him, "Master, who sinned first, this man or his parents, that he was born blind?" "Rabbi, did you read about these people whom Pilate killed at the Temple? What did they do to deserve such cruel fate?"

Jesus was angry with those exams, too; angry at the way we healthy, well-heeled, comfortable ones sit back and smugly, dispassionately discuss other people's pain, turn someone else's tragedy into a dormitory bull session on "Great Religious Ideas for Subconsciously Religious Intellectuals."

Now, Jesus is in the last week of his life, and he is met again with idle, speculative, cool questions: Do you advise paying taxes to Caesar (even though we're already bedded down with Caesar's coins)? Whose wife will this woman be in the afterlife (She's spent the whole of this life as someone's property, surely she will be property in the next life)? We would rather *talk* religion than *do* it.

Jesus replies by asking one question: What do *you* think of the Christ?

Jesus knows how our questions—our big, all-night, dormitory-bull-session questions—can deter us from the only real question (as far as he is concerned): What do *you* think of the Christ?

On another day, he gave his disciples a mid-term. "Who do people say that I am?"

"Oh, some say John the Baptist; two percent believe that you could be Elijah, those with incomes of over fifty thousand a year say that maybe you're Elisha or some other prophet."

Then Jesus sticks it to them: "Who do *you* say that I am?"

This is the only exam that means anything, when it's all said and done, according to Jesus. Not, What do you *think*? but, Where will you *commit*? Will you put your money down on me, trust me more than you trust your questions, and follow me down my narrow way? For you see, Jesus is on his way to put his money down, all of it, in the most expensive game a person can play—death—which is, of course, the game we're playing, too. But Jesus knows where his week will end and we don't—at least we don't act like it with our cool questions, as if we could permanently postpone life and death issues until we're back for our fortieth reunion.

This may be why Luke ends Jesus' final exam with the story of the widow's mite. Jesus looked at people passing the plate in the chapel, how the rich put their showy gifts in the plate. A poor widow only had two little coins to her name and she dropped in both. Jesus said, "She gave more than all the rest because she gave, not 10 percent off the top of her riches, but in her poverty, she gave everything she had. *All. Everything.*"

So just in case you thought Jesus was some professor who asks for nothing more of you than an open mind and three hours a week, remember he tells you what he's really after—everything that makes up your whole life, every red cent of it.

What think *you* of the Christ?

Isn't that typical of Jesus? You come asking him a straightforward question, only to have him ask you an even tougher question.

Whose exam is this anyway?

❖ Living with Life's Incompleteness

The LORD said to [Moses], "This is the land of which I swore to Abraham, to Isaac, and to Jacob, . . . I have let you see it with your eyes, but you shall not cross over there." (Deuteronomy 34:4)

Read Deuteronomy 34:1-8, 10-12

One of the joys of academic life is endings and beginnings. The last day of class. The first day of a new semester. The last hour of organic chemistry. The day of graduation.

How rare, in real life, is a clean break with the past. A major reason why it's fun to be on the faculty is that, unlike the rest of the world, there is always a day, here in early May, when *it's over*. As a young professor, I was told by an older professor that a university is a great place because "our failures keep graduating."

Things in the "real world" are not so neat. There are these histories we can't be rid of, these futures so uncertain.

On your day of graduation you are given a paper with your name upon it. All to assure you: It is over. This is it. Good-bye. *Adios.*

And what we hope is that you will look at that piece of paper, fondle the tassel, sing the alma mater, and really feel that you have accomplished something in school. But it is my sad duty to tell you, from what I have seen, most endings in the world are full of as much regret as satisfaction. In the world, there aren't many commencements, no slip of paper saying, "Your marriage has just ended, but you did an A– job as a husband. It's not your fault. *Adios.*" There is no one to say, "She's twenty-two now. Your parental responsibility is done. You were a 3.6 parent. It's over." In the real world, things are considerably more ragged, unfinished.

Beneath the notes of the alma mater, some of you will hear another refrain, called "Regret." I wish I had studied more. Why didn't I make more friends? We can hand you a diploma, march you in and then out, dress you in a funny flat hat, give you the illusion that you've actually cleared a hurdle, won the race, but things may be a good deal more ragged, unfinished, than we admit.

On Sundays, after I'm done preaching in chapel, after I've blended into the woodwork behind the second sopranos, I often look up to the stained-glass window high above and across from where I sit. I sit across from the Moses window. Surrounding a stark, towering Moses, are scenes from his life—Moses raised by royalty, Moses the defender of the oppressed, Moses the liberator, the lawgiver, the leader of Israel out of bondage to the Promised Land.

But somehow—at about 11:45 on Sunday, when I'm finished preaching and again tucked safely behind the second sopranos—the sun highlights one Moses scene more than the rest. It's the last scene—Moses held back from entering the Promised Land. God let Moses get to the door but not go over the threshold with his people. He never got to the Promised Land. Whether or not the stained-glass artist intended to force the preacher to ponder that scene, week-in-week-out, I know not. But it works. When I look at the end of Moses' life, I am reminded of our own.

There is much unfulfillment in this life, a great deal of life spent on the verge, at the door but not over the threshold, tethered to yesterday, unable to possess tomorrow. For me, for the second sopranos, we must, like Moses, come to terms with the incompleteness.

Moses led Israel out of Egyptian slavery, through the wilderness. Moses taught Israel the commands of God, interceded when Israel broke those commandments. Moses is therefore rightly called "servant of God" (Deuteronomy 34:5). If anyone should be going into the Promised Land, it ought to be Moses. The Deuteronomist implies that Moses violated God's law, but nothing really explains the tragedy of this last scene of Moses' life.

Moses lived 120 years and even, having lived almost two of our lifetimes, his life was unfinished. The burial place of Israel's greatest leader is unknown, unmarked, unremembered. As Elie Wiesel says of Moses' death, "Nobody knows his resting place. The people of the mountains situate it in the valley. The people of the valley situate it in the mountains. . . . Nobody was present at his death" (*Messengers of God*, pp. 204-5).

How fitting of Martin Luther King, Jr. to evoke this story in his last sermon. "I've been to the mountain. I've seen the Promised Land. Even if I don't get there with you. I've been to the mountaintop." King died outside the Promised Land of racial justice.

We want stories with happy endings. Boy gets girl; girl gets boy. They live happily ever after.

We love clean endings. Satisfying last scenes. Conclusive commencements.

But this is the Bible, this is life, not the movies. Things are messier in the Bible, messier in life. I have listened to the Bible and heard a word from Deuteronomy about unfinished business called our lives.

As a parent, I can tell you that the most important parental virtue is patience. Sometimes we parents just die for things to go ahead and work out in our children's lives.

A few years ago, Susan Litwin wrote *The Postponed Generation*. Young adults today, says Litwin, are not growing up, they are postponing adulthood into their late twenties. They graduate from prestigious colleges, not marching into the future, but meandering through unending adolescence, unable to make commitments, to leave home, afraid to put their money down on a future. Litwin names this national phenomenon of young adults—postponement.

Why? One of the reasons, says Litwin, is that your generation is suspicious of risk. Is her analysis fair? She says that your lives have been predictable, that so many things have worked out well for you that we have unintentionally deluded you into thinking that it is possible to plan and organize your life in such a way that all things will work out well.

So you postpone marriage longer than any previous generation, waiting for the perfect job, the absolutely right person, the two high performance cars, 2.3 children.

Alas, this is not life. Ask Moses. Life is an accumulation of decisions that could have been made differently, baggage called regret, faces you will not see again, words that came out wrong, things that don't work out as planned. Most of us don't spend much time thinking about it, and that's good, for accumulated regret, obsessive second guessing, leads to moral paralysis. People at forty "close doors more slowly."

I would like to tell Litwin, from what I have observed of you, that your generation is not so much paralyzed with caution, rather you are acutely aware of limits. Ecological, political, economic limits. Compared to your parents' generation of early Aquarian optimism, your awareness of limits may be a virtue. The challenge? *How to live with limits without paralysis.*

"In high school, I thought I could do anything I wanted to do," he said. "Four years of college has wised me up."

One of my jobs is officiating at weddings. And when I ask what a person is waiting for, on what basis he or she will finally decide to get married, the most frequent response is, "I'm trying to decide if this is the right person."

I now can say, after extensive observation, that's the wrong question. If getting married is a matter of finding the "right person" at twenty-three, so what? At twenty-four you will find that you are living with a very different person. That person has changed; and, of course, so have you. If marriage is about living with the right person, then what do you do? This is the reason that the church has never asked people getting married if they were certain they had the right person. All we ask is your willingness to risk with *this* person, even in the moments when this person is not right, for better for worse, richer or poorer. The willingness to risk commitment, through life's successes and regrets, is enough for togetherness.

Knowing that we live few stories with completely satisfying conclusions and utterly happy endings can be a step toward wisdom. So my word to you is, relax, *you don't have to get it right*. You can go ahead and live, not knowing how it will all turn out, not having to make it all turn out. Go ahead, venture, even if you don't arrive where you planned. Sometimes, the trip itself is more interesting than its destination. Go ahead, bet your life on someone, even with second thoughts, have children, even when the ones you get aren't the ones you thought you wanted.

Moses could tell us. Only God knows where it all leads, what it finally means. *We* are the story God writes. God only knows. So we can go ahead and commence with life in the conviction that God really does put us to good purposes, even though we may not see clearly, even though we may not enter the promised land of concrete results and visible fulfillment in our exodus from here to there.

And whether you achieve all your goals, make progress, arrive at your planned destinations, travel with the right people or not, here is the promise: As with Moses, *God goes with you.*